RESIDENCE MUNICH

OFFICIAL GUIDE

Edited by
HERBERT BRUNNER
GERHARD HOJER
LORENZ SEELIG
and
SABINE HEYM

1999
Bayerische Verwaltung der staatlichen Schlösser,
Gärten und Seen, München

The present English edition of the Official Guide to the Munich Residence corresponds to the German edition of the Official Guide from 1996.
The 1996 edition of the Official Guide is based on the text prepared by Herbert Brunner in 1971, which is an abbreviated version of the 1966 Guide written by Hans Thoma and Herbert Brunner. In the 1975, 1982 and 1986 editions, the Guide was augmented by Gerhard Hojer (overall editing and pictorial section as well as texts for the Silver Chamber and the Porcelain Chambers of the 19th century in 1975 and for the »Königsbau« in 1982), Horst H. Stierhof (Stone and Treves Rooms in 1975), Elmar D. Schmid (Green Gallery in 1975) and Lorenz Seelig (Imperial Hall, Four White Horses Hall and Imperial Staircase in 1986). The 1990 edition of the Guide was revised and the text partly altered by Sabine Heym.

Photographs: Bayerische Verwaltung der staatlichen Schlösser, Gärten und Seen, except for Figures 8, 29 (Claus Hansmann, Stockdorf), Figures 23, 24, 33 (Fabbri, Milan), Figure 30 (W. Chr. v. d. Mülbe, Dachau).

Translated by Ingrid Taylor
Revised by Sabine Glaser and Victoria J. Avery

Previous German-language editions of the Official Guide to the Residence Museum, Munich:

Adolf Feulner: Kleiner Führer durch das Residenzmuseum in München. Munich 1920 (further editions [2]1920, [3]1920)
Adolf Feulner: Residenzmuseum in München. Kleiner Führer. Munich-Berlin-Leipzig [4]1921 (further editions [5]1921, [6]1922, [7]1922, [8]1925: substantially altered edition, [9]after 1925)
Hans Thoma and Heinrich Kreisel: Residenz München. Amtlicher Führer. Munich 1937
Hans Thoma: Residenzmuseum München. Munich 1958 (further editions 1960, 1963, 1965)
Hans Thoma and Herbert Brunner: Residenzmuseum München. Munich 1966 (substantially expanded edition)
Herbert Brunner: Residenzmuseum München. Kurzführer. Munich 1971 (further edition 1972 with a new commentary on the Treves Rooms, Stone Rooms, Green Gallery. Munich 1973)
Herbert Brunner and Gerhard Hojer: Residenz München. Munich 1975 (further editions 1976 and 1979; 1982: expanded edition)
Herbert Brunner, Gerhard Hojer and Lorenz Seelig: Residenz München. Munich 1986 (further expanded edition: 1990)
Herbert Brunner, Gerhard Hojer, Lorenz Seelig and Sabine Heym: Residenz München. München 1996

CONTENTS

ARCHITECTURAL HISTORY

1255   Bavarian land partition. Duke Ludwig the Severe (reigned 1253-1294) moves his court from Landshut to Munich. Expansion of the "Old Court" on the north-eastern corner of the then city wall. Expansion and renovation of this oldest Munich princely seat under Duke Ludwig IV the Bavarian (Duke 1294, German King 1314, Roman Emperor 1328, died in 1347).

1385   Erection of the "Neuveste" (new citadel, originally conceived primarily as refuge), a new ruler's seat, in the north-eastern corner of the expanded city wall under the Dukes *Stephan III* and his brothers *Friedrich and Johann* (1375-1392).

1500   Expansion of the "Neuveste" between 1470 and 1500 to an extensive four-winged moated castle.
The "Neuveste" was gradually incorporated into superstructures erected in the following centuries. Small sections under the Apothecary Courtyard and under the eastern wing of the Banquet Hall structure are still preserved today.
The building activity from the 16th century onwards is marked by the character of its royal builders from the Wittelsbach dynasty.

Wilhelm IV, Duke 1508-1550; married Jacobäa Maria of Baden in 1522
Renovation of the eastern wing of the "Neuveste" by Ludwig Halder in 1540.

Albrecht V, Duke 1550-1579; married Anna of Austria in 1546

Erection of the Antiquarium (1568-1571) after designs by Jacopo Strada and Simon Zwitzel. Erection of a wing north of the "Jägergassl". Installation of the St. George Hall in the "Neuveste" from 1559 to 1572 under Wilhelm Egkl, opening of the bastions to arcades (not preserved). Layout of the rose garden to the east of the "Neuveste" (not preserved). Erection of a pleasure house in the garden near the "Neuveste", probably by Wilhelm Egkl in 1565 to 1567 (not preserved).

Wilhelm V, reigning Duke 1579-1597, died in 1626; married Renata of Lorraine in 1568

Ballroom between the "Neuveste" and the Antiquarium (approximately on the site of the present Old Residence Theatre), Widow's Building on the Schwabinger Gasse from 1580 to 1581 (not preserved). Grotto Courtyard Complex from 1581 to 1586 under the supervision of Friedrich Sustris. Black Hall Complex built. Richer decoration of the Antiquarium from 1581 to 1600.

Maximilian I, Duke 1598, Elector 1623, died in 1651; married Elisabeth of Lorraine in 1595 and Maria Anna of Austria in 1635.

Hans Krumper, Court Art Director. Extensive expansion of the Residence layout (Architects Heinrich Reiffenstuel and Heinrich Schön the Elder): Ground floor rooms on the Residenzgasse (accommodating today among other suites the Sacred Vestments Rooms) about 1600. New Court Chapel 1601-1603 (enlarged in 1630). Rich Chapel in 1607. Beginning of the Fountain Courtyard enclosure with the "Khürngang" (Antler Corridor) parallel to the Antiquarium, gable structures of the narrow courtyard sides, clock tower. Toward the west, expansion of the Court Ladies Building, part of which had been erected previously under Albrecht V, parallel to the northern end of the Grotto Courtyard enclosure, bordering the former "Jägergassl" (today the Chapel Courtyard). About 1612-1616 Imperial Courtyard Complex to the east, west and north (Imperial Stairway, Imperial Hall, Four White Horses Hall). Charlotte Corridor 1613-1615 and the (no longer extant) large Stag Corridor connect the Residence with the remnant of the "Neuveste" in the north-east. The original decoration of the "Steinzimmer" (Stone Rooms), "Trierzimmer" (Treves Rooms), and Imperial Stairway is preserved, as is that of the Imperial and the Four White Horses Hall (reconstructed). 1613 to 1620 layout of the court garden in the area north of the Residence.

Ferdinand Maria, Elector 1651-1679; married Henriette Adelaide of Savoy in 1652

Decoration of the suites for the electoral couple from 1658. The so-called Papal Rooms (refurnished 1666-1667) from the apartment of the Electress Henriette Adelaide are preserved. Golden Hall Complex (1666-1667) in the south of the west front as connection to the Widow's Building. The Residence fire in 1674 destroyed parts of the Stone Rooms and the Imperial Hall Complex. Partial restoration until 1680.

Maximilian II Emanuel, Elector 1679-1726; married Maria Antonia of Austria in 1685 and Therese Kunigunde of Poland in 1694

Renovation of the Grotto Courtyard tracts about 1680-1685 (Alexander and Summer Rooms). Remodelling of the Dressing Room in the Alexander Rooms into two cabinets: Dutch Cabinet and Music Cabinet (1693-1695). Final restoration of the Four White Horses Hall (1690-1694) and of the Stone Rooms (1694-1700). Cecilia Chapel (1693-1704). First rooms of the Rich Suite after plans by Joseph Effner in 1726.

Karl Albrecht, Elector 1726, Roman Emperor 1742, died in 1745; married Maria Amalia of Austria in 1722

Continuation of the renovation work by Joseph Effner. Residence fire in 1729 followed by redesigning of the damaged sections of the Rich Rooms until 1733 by François Cuvilliés the Elder; Ancestral Gallery (1726-1730) and the Green Gallery (as new wing projecting to the south with its own façade 1731-1733).

Max III Joseph, Elector 1745-1777; married Maria Anna of Saxony in 1747

Renovation of the Electoral Chambers above the Antiquarium by Johann Baptist Gunetzrhainer (1746-1748). Residence fire in 1750. Following this, construction of the (Old) Residence Theatre (1751-1753) by François Cuvilliés the Elder.

Karl Theodor, Elector of the Palatinate 1742, Elector of Bavaria 1777, died in 1799; married Elisabeth Auguste of Palatine-Sulzbach in 1742 and Maria Leopoldine of Austria-Este in 1795

Max IV Joseph, Elector 1799, King (Max I Joseph) 1806, died 1825; married Auguste Wilhelmine of Hesse-Darmstadt in 1785 and Karoline of Baden in 1797

Decoration of the Court Garden Rooms - in the area of

the renovated suite of the Imperial and the Four White Horses Hall - by Charles-Pierre Puille from 1799 to 1801 and Andreas Gärtner from 1801 to 1816. Decoration of the Council of State Chambers along the Residenzstraße in 1810. Remodelling of the Old Hercules Hall (today the Max Joseph Hall) in the Ladies' Building by Andreas Gärtner from 1814 to 1816. Charlotte Chambers 1814. Court and National Theatre by Karl von Fischer and Leo von Klenze from 1811 to 1825. Court Riding School by Leo von Klenze from 1817 to 1822.

Ludwig I, King 1825-1848, died in 1868; married Therese of Saxe-Hildburghausen in 1810

Demolition of the "Neuveste" and the Widows' Building. Erection of the new South Wing, the "Königsbau" (Royal Palace) from 1826 to 1835, the Court Church of All Saints from 1826 to 1837 and the north-facing Banquet Hall Building (with Throne Room and Ballroom) under Leo von Klenze from 1835 to 1847.

Maximilian II, King 1848-1864; married Marie of Prussia in 1842

Southern Winter Garden, between the "Königsbau" and the National Theatre, by Franz Jakob Kreuter and August von Voit in 1854 (no longer preserved).

Ludwig II, King 1864-1886

Dwelling apartment in the north-western pavilion by Eduard Riedel and Franz Seitz from 1866 to 1869 and the Second Winter Garden after plans by Eduard Riedel and Carl von Effner, from 1868 to 1871 (destroyed).

Luitpold, Prince Regent 1886-1912; married Auguste Ferdinande of Tuscany in 1877

Old Treasury 1897 by Julius Hofmann.

Ludwig III, King 1913-1918; married Maria Therese of Austria-Este in 1868

Free State of Bavaria

1920 Opening of the Residence Museum.

1944 War destruction.

1953 Opening of the concert hall built in the Banquet Hall Building (New Hercules Hall) in place of the destroyed Throne Room of Ludwig I.

1958 Reopening of the Old Residence Theatre (so-called Cuvilliés Theatre) now transferred into the "Apothecary Block".

1958 Reopening of the first section of the Residence circular tour including the Antiquarium, the Court Chapel, the Ancestral Gallery, the Papal Chambers, the Rich Rooms, the Nibelungen Halls and the Porcelain Chambers of the 18th century as well as reopening of the Treasury in new premises in the "Königsbau" (Royal Palace).

1966 Opening of the second section of the Residence circular tour including the Electoral Chambers, the Charlotte Chambers, the Court Garden Rooms and the Rich Chapel.

1973 Opening of the third section of the Residence circular tour including the Stone and Treves Rooms as well as the Green Gallery.

1974   Opening of the "Schlachtensäle" (Battle Halls) and
        Porcelain Chambers of the 19th century in the "Königs-
        bau" (Royal Palace) as well as of the Silver Chambers in
        the "Hartschiersaal" (Bodyguards' Hall) and the former
        Assembly Rooms of the Council of State.

1979   Restoration of the ceiling paintings of the Black Hall.

1980   Opening of the Royal Apartments in the "Königsbau"
        (Royal Palace). Restoration of the Imperial Courtyard.

1985   Opening of the Imperial Staircase, the Imperial Hall and
        the Four White Horses Hall as well as reopening of the
        Max Joseph Hall (formerly Old Hercules Hall) primarily
        used as concert and exhibition hall.

The Munich Residence as seat of the Wittelsbach rulers had
been a centre of the arts and sciences. After its restoration, it
once again became an abode of the muses and of the intellect.
The restoration work - planned from 1944 onwards - was substantially completed in 1985. In addition to the splendid rooms
from four centuries - including the Old Residence Theatre of
François Cuvilliés - and the collections of the Residence
Museum and the Treasury which are open to visitors, the Residence also houses the State Collection of Egyptian Art and the
State Coin Collection, as well as the Bavarian Academy of Sciences, the Bavarian Academy of Fine Arts, the Spanish Cul-
ture Institute and the Headquarters of the Max-Planck-
Gesellschaft. The great concerts in the New Hercules Hall and
in the Max Joseph Hall also make the Residence a centre of
Bavarian musical life.

EXTERIOR FAÇADES OF THE RESIDENCE

West Front (Residenzstrasse)

1612-1616, with two marble portals and marble niche of the "Patrona Boiariae" *(Fig. 2)*. - To the north, corner pavilion of the Banquet Hall Building from 1835 to 1842. - To the south, three axes of the "Golden Hall Tract" from 1666 to 1667 and narrow side of the "Königsbau" (Royal Palace) from 1826-1835.

Architectural painting

Renovated in 1958 from the 18th century originals.

Bronze sculptures

Works by Hans Krumper: Statue of the Blessed Virgin Mary as Patrona Boiariae (Patroness of Bavaria); cast in 1615 by Bartel Wenglein, chasing by Georg Maier; the marble pilaster aedicula with Eternal Light bears a dedication inscription dated 1616. - Reclining figures on the pediments of the portals about 1616 (allegories of the four cardinal virtues): On the northern portal "Wisdom" and "Justice", on the southern portal "Fortitude" and "Temperance". - Reliefs above the side doors of the portals: Escutcheons of Bavaria and Lorraine held by lions and griffins (Elisabeth, the first wife of Maximilian I, was a princess of Lorraine).

Works by Hubert Gerhard and Carlo Pallago, about 1594: Two pairs of lions (the emblematic reliefs on the shields were added by Hans Krumper in c. 1616).

"Königsbau" or Royal Palace (Max-Joseph-Platz)

Built from 1826 to 1835 by Leo von Klenze inspired by Florentine Renaissance palaces (Palazzo Pitti and Palazzo Rucellai). Yellowish rusticated sandstone with diamond-faceted square-cut masonry.

Banquet Hall Building (Court Garden front)

1835 to 1842 by Leo von Klenze inspired by North Italian Renaissance architecture (particularly that of Andrea Palladio). Behind the classical facade of the western section of the building are parts of the Residence erected by Maimilian after 1612; the eastern section was rebuilt by Leo von Klenze. On the central building: Stone sculptures by Ludwig Schwanthaler (two lions and the allegories of the then eight districts of Bavaria).

East Front (Marstallplatz)

Formerly a classical forum opposite the Royal Mews (Klenze, 1817-1822), consisting of the eastern corner of the Banquet Hall Building (Klenze, 1835-1842), the façade of the Court Church of All Saints (Klenze 1826-1837) and the echeloned east sides of the two theatres. Today obscured by installations.

RESIDENCE MUSEUM

1 Vestibule on the Royal Palace Courtyard

Ground floor hall in the wing of the Green Gallery by François Cuvilliés the Elder built in 1733. - At the right, entrance to the Old Treasury, built in 1897 from plans by Julius Hofmann, now serving as exhibition room.

Sculptures
Four carved figures, "Judgement of Paris", probably Munich about 1730.
Limewood, painted to simulate stone.

Four stone busts from an "Allegory of the Four Continents" (two representing Africa two Europe), by Charles de Groff, Munich 1768.
Multicoloured marble and stucco made to simulate marble.

Through the windows: View into the

"KÖNIGSBAU" COURTYARD

The western French doors provide a view onto the "Königs-bau" (Royal Palace) courtyard. From the later 16th century, the "Large Residence Garden" was located here. The erection of the Green Gallery Wing in 1733 split the garden into two halves.

Bronze sculptures
Two satyrs and four putti, ascribed to Carlo Pallago, Munich about 1576/78.

Two spring gods, probably Munich about 1630.

14

2 First Garden Hall

Sculptures

Male figure with bow and stag (Nimrod?) and female figure with mirror, probably by Dominicus Auliczek, Munich about 1771/72.

Limewood, painted to simulate stone. These served as models for the stone figures of Pluto and Proserpina in the Nymphenburg Palace park parterre.

Three stone busts from an "Allegory of the Continents" (two representing America and one of Asia), by Charles de Groff, Munich 1768.

Multicoloured marble and stucco made to simulate marble. Belonging with the four busts in the Vestibule (Room 1).

Knotwork tapestries

A large tapestry and two small tapestries with baroque garden scenes (rear wall), Savonnerie Manufactory Heidelberg, probably 1772-1775 by Peter Jesse.

Two tapestries with baroque garden scenes (narrow sides), Savonnerie Manufactory Mannheim, 1763-1768 by Stephan Boßmann.

Furniture

Console table (rear wall), Munich about 1723-1725, style of Joseph Effner.

Limewood, carved and gilded.

Two console tables (on the narrow sides), after a design by François Cuvilliés the Elder, probably carved by Wenzeslaus Miroffsky, Munich c. 1730.

Limewood, carved and gilded.

3 Second Garden Hall

Oil paintings

Thomas Christian Wink: Allegory of Spring, Munich, dated 1770.

Design for a pictorial tapestry of the Munich Gobelin Manufactory. The allegories of summer, autumn and winter have been lost.

Thomas Christian Wink: Flora and Pomona, Munich, probably about 1770.

Through the glazed French doors of the southern side: View toward the façade of the Green Gallery (erected in 1731-1733 by François Cuvilliés the Elder).

4 Ancestral Gallery   *Fig. 17*

Laid out in the late 16th century as a garden hall of the Large Residence Garden, the room was remodelled in 1726-1730, probably still under the supervision of Joseph Effner, into an ancestral gallery, and was magnificently decorated. Gilded and carved wall panelling by Wenzeslaus Miroffsky in 1729-1730. The 121 portraits depict the reigning rulers in Bavaria - principally the Wittelsbachs and their relatives. Some are variants of older models (from the studio of Jacopo Amigoni), while others are contemporary portraits of about 1730 (from the studio of George Desmarées). Others date from about 1760 to approximately 1913. In the middle, three large paintings from the studio of Jacopo Amigoni, showing the legendary first Bavarian duke Theodo as well as Emperor Charlemagne and Emperor Ludwig the Bavarian. In the middle of the window-wall, a drawing of the Wittelsbach family tree of 1730/31. Above the cavetto divided by consoles, a barrel vault with gilded stuccowork by Johann Baptist Zimmermann (1728-1730) and a central ceiling painting by Balthasar Augustin Albrecht (c. 1730): Reinstatement of the Order of the Knights of St. George by Elector Karl Albrecht in 1729. Formerly there were two ceiling pictures at the sides (Coronation of Emperor Ludwig the Bavarian in 1328 in Rome, Investiture of Theodo with the Duchy of Bavaria after 508) (destroyed). Overall, the programme of the Ancestral Gallery presents Karl Albrecht's claim to the imperial throne.

5   Porcelain Cabinet

The room constructed in 1730-1733 from a design by François Cuvilliés the Elder, was originally the Electoral Treasury; it was furnished in 1911 as a porcelain cabinet (for the most part, the porcelain pieces are the property of the Wittelsbach State Foundation for Art and Science). - White panelling with glazed wall cabinets and flush-mounted mirrors; the gilded carving of the doors, the cabinets and mirrors and the continuous wainscot by Joachim Dietrich 1733. The gilded ceiling stuccowork by Johann Baptist Zimmermann.

Porcelain pieces in the wall cabinets
Entrance wall: Products from several Manufactories: Sèvres (bird motif service 1759), Vienna (creamers), Würzburg (mythological figures).

Long wall on both sides: Frankenthal Manufactory with works by Johann Wilhelm Lanz, Johann Friedrich Lück, Konrad Linck, Adam Bauer.

Long wall, middle: Meissen Manufactory with works from the second half of the 18th century.

End wall, middle: Nymphenburg Manufactory with pieces from the "Pearl Service" of 1792-1795, ornamental vases by Dominicus Auliczek 1777, allegories of the arts and sciences 1777 and group "The Listener at the Fountain" by Franz Anton Bustelli.

End wall, at the side: Sèvres and other French manufactories from the second half of the 18th century (figures in biscuit porcelain); Vienna (creamers).

Porcelain on the wall consoles
Predominantly biscuit vases by Adam Clair, Nymphenburg.

Furnishings
Two console tables, after a design by François Cuvilliés the Elder, Munich about 1730.
Limewood, carved and gilded. On them:

Two Meissen flute vases with Hoeroldt-painting.

Chandelier, middle of the 18th century

IN THE CIRCULAR TOUR I, ROOM 6 (GROTTO COURT-YARD) NOW FOLLOWS. CIRCULAR TOUR II BRANCHES OFF HERE INTO ROOM 82 (PORCELAIN CHAMBERS OF THE 18TH CENTURY, PAGE 134).

CIRCULAR TOUR I

6   Grotto Courtyard   *Fig. 1*

Duke Wilhelm V had a four-wing building with richly decorated interior garden erected by Friedrich Sustris from 1581 to 1586 adjoining the Antiquarium. Despite later changes, this "secret pleasure and residence garden" still exudes the joyous spirit of southern Renaissance gardens.

Façades

The original elevation of the courtyard with an arched hall on each of the two narrow sides is preserved only on the east side (where the visitor is standing). On the ground floor there is an arcade with seven arches supported by slender Tuscan columns of Adnet marble. On the upper floor between the windows, niches with casts taken from statues of the second half of the 16th century (see Room 8). The upper story of the west wing, whose roof additionally carries a transverse gable, is the same as the upper storey of the east wing. Under François Cuvilliés the Elder, the longitudinal walls of the courtyard were provided with new curtain façades in c. 1730; at the same time, the arched hall of the west wing was closed and divided by pilasters to match the walls of the longitudinal sides.

Bronze sculptures in the garden

Perseus Fountain, by Hubert Gerhard, Munich about 1590. Initial design by Friedrich Sustris.

Four putti with fabulous beasts, ascribed to Carlo Pallago, Munich about 1576/78.

Hall

The Grotto Hall was largely destroyed in 1944. From 1956 to 1958, the columns, vaults and stuccoed frame-members were reconstructed according to the old model and the partially preserved paintings in the arch bays were restored (overall design by Friedrich Sustris, executed probably between 1586 and 1589, mainly by Alessandro Paduano, Antonio Maria Viani, Peter Candid and Antonio Ponzano). - The grotto complex encrusted with tuff, crystals, colourful mussel shells, etc. conceals the north-west corner of the Antiquarium which projects here. In the arch there is a fountain niche supported by caryatids. It is closed at the top by the Bavarian ducal coat of arms held by Moors.

Sculptures in the Hall
Bronze statue: Mercury (gilded), attributed to Hubert Gerhard, 1587/88.

Marble busts in the niches: Satyrs, paniscs, a silenus, an allegory of sleep and an allegory of autumn; reproductions of antique sculptures made in the second half of the 16th and the first half of the 17th century.

7   Antiquarium (Hall of Antiquities)   *Fig. 3*

This is the most important and - at a length of 66 m - also the largest secular Renaissance room of the 16th century north of the Alps. Created under Duke Albrecht V between 1568 and 1571 by Jacopo Strada and Simon Zwitzel as a hall for the ducal collection of antiques, it was remodelled in 1581 to 1600 under the supervision of Friedrich Sustris into a banquet hall. Until 1599, the upper storey housed the ducal library.

Under Sustris, the floor in the middle section was lowered, and the ceiling and window reveals were given their present painted decoration. The new rich ornamentation can be attributed to the workshop of Carlo Pallago. The dais for holding princely banquets was also made during the reign of Wilhelm V. The endwalls were redesigned - with a fireplace and with portal fixtures in red stucco (to simulate marble) - during the reign of Maximilian I.

The extremely long and relatively low hall is covered with a mighty barrel vault, intersected on the longitudinal axes by 17 window lunettes (with terra cotta laurel-branch framings). Vault and window reveals after an overall design by Friedrich Sustris decorated with paintings by Peter Candid (atelier), Antonio Ponzano, Hans Donauer (Thonauer) the Elder, et al; 16 allegories of fame and of the virtues in the crowning of the vault; pairs of putti in the vault spandrels; and grotesque decorations with views of old Bavarian towns in the lunettes and window reveals.

102 views of cities, markets, castles and palaces of the then Duchy of Bavaria by Hans Donauer the Elder, et al from 1586 to 1590.

Right side (viewed from the entrance by the Grotto Courtyard):

1. Abensberg, Grünwald, Fürstenfeldbruck. 2. Moosburg, Vohburg, Kranzberg. 3. Landshut, Kraiburg, Kösching. 4. Furth im Wald, Nannhofen, Geisenhausen. 5. Grafenau, Graisbach, Wartenberg. 6. Dietfurt, Neurandsberg, Chamerau. 7. Burghausen, Kirchberg, Natternberg. 8. Straubing, Vilsbiburg, Mainburg. 9. Ingolstadt, Bad Aibling, Hals. 10. Wasserburg am Inn, Schwindegg, Auerburg. 11. Landsberg, Teisbach, Markt Schwaben. 12. Schärding, Ried im Innkreis, Reisbach. 13. Bad Reichenhall, Friedburg, Wildshut. 14. Braunau am Inn, Haidau, Diessenstein. 15. Dingolfing, Viechtach, Wolnzach. 16. Schongau, Hengersberg, Kötzting. 17. Friedberg, Bärnstein, Regen.

Left side (back from the exit wall):

1. Pfaffenhofen an der Ilm, Isareck, Starnberg. 2. Wemding, Uttendorf, Haag. 3. Vilshofen, Mitterfels, Murnau. 4. Landau an der Isar, Pähl, Mörmoosen. 5. Rain, Eggmühl, Hohenschwangau. 6. Traunstein, Eggenfelden, Donaustauf (captions exchanged). 7. Aichach, Neumarkt-St. Veit, Rosenheim. 8. Neustadt an der Donau, Griesbach im Rottal, Rottenburg an der Laaber. 9. Kelheim, Trostberg, Bad Tölz. 10. Erding, Blutenburg, Marquartstein. 11. Schrobenhausen, Frontenhausen, Rauhenlechsberg. 12. Deggendorf, Schönberg, Sattelpeilnstein. 13. Osterhofen, Mauerkirchen, Valley. 14. Weilheim, Mering, Leonsberg. 15. München, Kling, Bad Abbach. 16. Stadtamhof, Geisenfeld, Riedenburg. 17. Neuötting, Wolfratshausen, Dachau.

The damage of 1944 (collapse of the bays of the middle vault) was repaired by 1958 and the paintings in these sections were restored. The paintings of the vault crown, which had been largely destroyed were replaced by a later version by the Peter

Candid studio probably made about 1615/1620 which, painted on wooden panels, had fortunately been perserved.

The two longitudinal walls of the hall are divided by wall pillars, which are adorned with niches and terra cotta capitals. Each wall section thus holds six busts. A large part of the sculptures, mostly heads, were purchased by art agents of Duke Albrecht V in 1566 and 1567 in Italy, particularly in Venice and Rome. Many of these heads were inserted into busts carved in munich in 1572-1580 (Jordan Prechenfelder, Hans Ernhofer). Among the heads themselves are many which imitate antique exemplars, particularly of the 16th century, but also of the 17th and 18th centuries. Of the genuinely antique works - some of which have been heavily restored - a few are Imperial Roman copies after Greek originals, but the majority are Roman portrait-busts. The inscriptions beneath the busts date from the building period of the Antiquarium and, except for a few, cannot be considered as historically accurate.

On the two narrow sides, fireplace and portal superstructures, each framed by niches with life-sized antique figures and busts, at the fireplace, the Bavarian coat of arms with ducal coronet and Golden Fleece.

Two sideboards
Probably Munich about 1590, after design by Friedrich Sustris.
Walnut casing, spruce interior.

In front of the music platform and the estrade:
Pedestals with architectural views in scagliola, Wilhelm Pfeiffer (Fistulator), Munich about 1630-1640.
During banquets, the ducal table was placed on the estrade in front of the fireplace.

8 Octagon

Octagonal vaulted room with seven oval windows. Stucco about 1600-1610.

Sculptures

Five figures composed of antique marble fragments with heads (mostly of stucco) in imitation of classical antique style, primarily from the 18th century.

The figures previously stood in the niches of the upper story of the west wall of the Grotto Courtyard (duplicates are located there now, see Room 6).

Portrait head of a philosopher in marble, Roman, second century AD.

9 Gateway

Western ground floor section of the Black Hall complex erected about 1580.

Through the gate opening: View into the

FOUNTAIN COURTYARD

The elongated octagon of this outdoor festive hall *(cover picture)* originated about 1612 to 1616 from building sections already standing as well as newly built sections.

On the north-western narrow side the Residence Tower erected in 1612-1615 (destroyed 1944; remade by 1957) with (renovated) sundial and mechanical clock. In the foreground facade of the "Broad Stairs" with high scroll gable crowned by obelisks and a bust. Old engravings permitted an accurate restoration of the facade frescoes in 1959/60.

The Wittelsbach Fountain

The fountain honours the Palatine Count Otto von Wittelsbach, the first Duke of Bavaria from the Wittelsbach Dynasty, whose bronze effigy stands on the base adorned with the monogram ME (the initials of the donors Maximilian I and Elisabeth). Hubert Gerhard made the figure which was completed in 1592/93.

The bronze figures on the rim of the quatrefoil-shaped basin (the four elements represented by Vulcan, Juno, Neptune and Ceres, as well as four river gods, four Triton children and four groups of fabulous beasts) are copies of originals by Hubert Gerhard and his studio from 1586/88. The bronze originals came from another complex, but were documented in this arrangement as early as in 1613 (the fountain architecture itself was altered in the course of the 17th century). The statue of Otto von Wittelsbach (see Room 113) is likewise a bronze copy of the original.

10 Room with Hercules relief

Groined vault with post-Gothic stellar configurations.

Marble relief
Reclining Hercules with two-handled vase, first century BC or first century AD.

Bust
Male head, end of the first/beginning of the second century AD (probably eastern Mediterranean), in imitation of models from the first half of the 5th century BC; inserted in a Renaissance bust.

11 Corridor in front of the stairs to the Black Hall

The rich stuccowork of the vault originates from the period about 1610-1620: Coffered work, modelled ornaments and masks.

Paintings
Two naval battle scenes (Tunis), Netherlandish about 1620.

12 Stairs to the Black Hall

Wide staircase in two returning flights with barrel and groined vaulting about 1600. Stuccowork c. 1610.

On the middle landing:

Two monumental busts of Emperors Hadrian and Nero, Renaissance copies from Roman originals.

An imposing portal of black stucco marble (renovated in part) provides the entrance to the Black Hall.

13 Black Hall   *Fig. 4*

The Black Hall adjoining the Antiquarium complex to the east dates to the era of Duke Wilhelm V, about 1590.

The name, recorded as early as the 17th century, derives from the huge black stucco marble portals. The ceiling painting by Hans Werl probably in 1602 (restored in 1669 by Caspar Amort) appears to open the coffin-lid ceiling to reveal an illusionistic two-storey architecture with gallery and oval tambour dome (destroyed in 1944, reconstructed in 1979 by Karl Manninger). The four stucco marble portals, probably erected under the direction of Hans Krumper about 1623, were destroyed in the war and are now replaced by copies which contain the preserved fragments from the orignials. A similarly richly decorated fireplace adorned the west wall from c. 1623 until 1944 (when it was destroyed).

Paintings:

Nikolaus Prugger(?) after Joachim von Sandrart: Elector Maximilian I, between 1641 and 1650.

Probably Munich c. 1645/50: Maria Anna of Austria, second wife of Maximilian I.

Engelhard de Pee(?): Duke Maximilian I as Hereditary Prince, about 1594/95.

Probably Munich about 1600 under French influence: Elisabeth of Lorraine, first wife of Maximilian I.

Engelhard de Pee: Duke Wilhelm V and his wife Renata of Lorraine, about 1590.

Probably Munich, (after) 1613: Magdalena of Bavaria, Duchess of Palatine Neuburg.

Engelhard de Pee: Albrecht VI, the Leuchtenberger, 1601(?).

Munich, about 1620: Duke Maximilian I.

Engelhard de Pee(?): Duke Philipp Wilhelm, Cardinal and Bishop of Regensburg, 1597/98.

Light fixtures
Chandelier, probably Paris, beginning of the 19th century.
Gilt bronze.

Six wall brackets, second quarter of the 19th century.
Gilt bronze.

14, 14a-14g Rooms in the "Königsbau" (Royal Palace)

King Ludwig I of Bavaria (reigned from 1825 to 1848) had the "Königsbau" (Royal Palace) erected from designs made by the architect Leo von Klenze to form the southern termination of the entire Residence complex. The apartments of the king and of the queen were located on the first floor; they were largely destroyed in World War II, but by 1980 were largely restored to their former grandeur. (Rooms 115-127).

14 Yellow Staircase

Monumental entrance to the apartments of King Ludwig I in the main floor of the "Königsbau" (Royal Palace). Restored from 1956 to 1960. The flight of stairs has a barrel vault; the original vault height of the apsis shell above the landing on the lower beginning of the staircase was no longer able to be reached.

Sculpture
Venus Italica by Antonio Canova, 1804-1811.
White marble.

Furnishings
Two vases and two pylons, probably Manufactory of Joseph von Utzschneider, Saargemünd, early 19th century.
Red-brown artificial stone compound with gilt bronze mounts.

14a-14c "Schlachtensäle" (Battle Halls)

Formerly First and Second Antechambers and Service Hall for the King's Apartment (see p. 195 et seq.). The murals after designs by Ludwig M. Schwanthaler and Julius Schnorr von Carolsfeld depicted scenes from the Argonaut legend, the poems of Hesiod and the Homeric hymns. Since these rooms were completely destroyed, only the floors and ceilings could be reconstructed in imitation of their former appearance. In place of the lost murals, were hung fourteen large battle paintings in 1974, which came from the so-called Battle Hall in the

Court Garden complex of the Residence. That hall, which was likewise destroyed in World War II, had been built as banquet hall for officers of the Bavarian Army; around its walls, Ludwig I had inserted fourteen paintings with battle scenes from the Napoleonic campaigns from 1805 to 1815 in some of which he had participated as Crown Prince. Although he had commissioned these battle pictures as early as 1807 - which were to be painted from sketches made at the battlefields - they were not completed until the late 1830s.

14a First Battle Hall (former First Antechamber of the King)

Paintings

Peter Heß: Storming of the Bodenbühl near Bad Reichenhall (1805), painted in 1829.

Wilhelm von Kobell: Surrender of Brieg (1807), painted in 1809/10.

Copy after Joseph Stieler: King Ludwig I in coronation robes with the Bavarian crown insignia, painted about 1826.

Furniture

Four armchairs, Munich about 1830.
Carved and painted white and gold. Blue silk covering renewed. Additional chairs from the ensemble in Room 117.

14b Second Battle Hall (former Second Antechamber of the King)

Paintings

Wilhelm von Kobell: Siege of Breslau (1806/07), painted in 1810/11.

Wilhelm von Kobell: Battle near Arnhofen (in the vicinity of Abensberg in Lower Bavaria) (1809), painted in 1813.

Wilhelm von Kobell: Battle near Eggmühl (1809), painted in 1809/10.

Wilhelm von Kobell: Battle near Wagram (1809), painted in 1811.

Peter Heß: Encounter near Wörgl (1809), painted in 1832/33 *(Fig. 40)*.

Wilhelm von Kobell: Battle near Polozk (1812), painted in 1813.

On the window pier:
Joseph Stieler: King Ludwig I in his coronation robes, 1826.

Furniture
18 chairs and three console tables, Munich 1834/35.
Carved, painted white and gold. Renewed red velvet covering. From the Service Hall of the king (see Room 14c).

Two alabaster vases with equestrian Cupids, about 1820.

Large porcelain vase in crater form, Nymphenburg Manufactory, from a model by Johann Peter Melchior; the portrait of Crown Prince Ludwig painted by Christian Adler in 1820 from a painting by Joseph Stieler of 1816.

Two reproductions of the Trajan and of the Antoninus Pius Column in Rome, by Benjamin Ludwig Jollage and Wilhelm Hopfgarten, Rome probably about 1817.
Gilt bronze. Probably presented to Max I Joseph on the occasion of the signing of the Concordat in 1817.

Twelve-branch chandelier with crowning Bacchus figure from the former Dining Hall in the "Königsbau" (Royal Palace), made by the Polytechnic-Institute of Nuremberg about 1833-1835.
Gilt bronze.

14c Third Battle Hall (former Service Hall of the King)

Paintings
Albrecht Adam: Battle of Borodino (1812), painted in 1832-1835.

Carl Wilhelm von Heideck: Skirmish at Brienne (1814), painted after 1835.

Peter Heß: Engagement at Bar-sur-Aube (1814), painted in 1838.

Peter Heß: Battle at Arcis-sur-Aube, right wing (1814), painted in 1816.

Peter Heß: Battle at Arcis-sur-Aube, left wing (1814), painted in 1821-1826.

Dietrich Monten: Battle at Saarbrücken (1815), painted probably about 1835/40.

On the window pier:
Marianne Kuerzinger: King Max I as General of the Infantry, 1806.

Furnishings
24 chairs and three console tables, probably from a design by Andreas Gärtner, Munich about 1810.

Carved and gilded, red silk coverings renovated from a contemporary model. The ensemble comes from the Council of State Chambers of Max I Joseph (see p. 158)

Mantelpiece clock with group of the Oath of the Horatii, probably by Claude Galle, Paris about 1805, after the painting of Jacques-Louis David from 1784.
Gray marble and gilt bronze.

Six-branched chandelier with 54 candlesticks, Alexander May, probably from a design by Leo von Klenze, made in the bronze foundry of Carl von Moy, Munich about 1833-1835.
Gilt bronze. The chandelier is part of the original decor of the room.

Two table candlesticks, probably Munich about 1842 (probably from the Banquet Hall Building).
Gilt bronze.

14d-14g Porcelain Chambers (European porcelain of the 19th century)

The rooms located at the rear of the Royal State Chambers were set up in 1974 to display the porcelain services of the 19th century. Until World War II these had been displayed together with the 18th century European porcelain in the Porcelain Chambers of the Grotto Courtyard (Room 82-88). At that time due to space restrictions only a selection was shown; now, for the first time, they can be displayed in their entirety.

In contrast to the porcelain services of the 18th century, whose decoration was usually purely ornamental, porcelain in the 19th century became increasingly embellished with pictorial motifs. The vessel shapes are correspondingly plainer and the ornamental decoration becomes the frame for the coloured pictures.

In addition to the Royal Porcelain Manufactory of Nymphen-burg, the manufactory in Berlin and French manufactories also delivered large porcelain services due to the family and political ties of the Wittelsbach dynasty.

14d French Manufactories

Because of the alliance of King Max I Joseph of Bavaria with Napoleon, the official art of Bavaria necessarily became dependent on the prevailing artistic taste in France in the early 19th century, the Empire style. At court dinners, porcelain from the French manufactories was preferred. In 1810, King Max I Joseph received two large services from the Sèvres Manufactory as a present from Napoleon. Queen Caroline ordered porcelain items from the same manufactory.

Right detached display case and wall-mounted display cases on the entrance wall, the right window wall and the right narrow side:

Dessert-service with colour-printed decoration, showing among other subjects scenes from Roman history and mythology, and also Parisian city views and views of English country houses as well as Italian and Swiss views. Stone-Coquerel and Legros d'Anisy Manufactory, Paris about 1810/20.

Middle detached display case and two further wall display cases on the window wall:

"Service encyclopédique": Farmers, craftsmen, Orientals, soldiers (Cossacks), games, sport, hunting and equestrian scenes. Sèvres Manufactory 1804-1808; pictorial sections in sepia painting by Jacques-François Joseph Swebach called Fontaine. The "Service encyclopédique" was presented in 1810 by Emperor Napoleon to King Max I Joseph.

Left detached display case and wall display cases on the left narrow side and the left window wall:
Service with floral decoration, Sèvres Manufactory 1808/09. The service was ordered by Queen Caroline in Sèvres in 1808; in 1810 the Emperor Napoleon made a gift of 24 flower plates of this service to the royal couple.

Small Cabinet

At the left: Three washbasins with coast landscapes, Paris, first half of the 19th century. - Parts of a table-service for King Max I. Joseph of Bavaria, Dagoty Manufactory, Paris about 1810. - Seven plates and a bowl, Montereau Manufactory, Louis Lebeuf, (after) 1834.

In the middle: Parts of a table-service for King Max I Joseph of Bavaria, Dagoty Manufactory, Paris, about 1810. - Six vases with gilt bronze mount and portraits of the family of King Joachim Murat by Raffaele Giovine, Naples early 19th century.

At the right: Five vases, Ludwigsburg Manufactory about 1800. - Putto writing the name Karl Theodor, biscuit porcelain, probably Dihl et Guerhard Manufactory, Paris about 1795.

14e Nymphenburg Manufactory

Made in 1792-1795, the so-called "Pearl Service" (displayed in Room 86 and in Room 5) was the first large table-service to be ordered from the Nymphenburg Manufactory by the Wittelsbach, the ruling house of Bavaria. The last large court-commission to the Manufactory was the "Onyx Service", which King Ludwig I ordered in 1835 and which derives its name from its purple-coloured ("Pompeiian red") background. The architect Friedrich von Gärtner supplied the designs; he had been the manufactory's artistic director since 1822. The service, comprising 717 pieces, was completed in 1848.

Detached display case:
Vessels which imitate antique forms and show reproductions of marble sculptures in the Munich Glyptothek in grisaille painting on purple-coloured ("onyx") background *(Fig. 39).* - Matching plates without figural painting and parts of a similar service with meander rim.

Longitudinal wall:
Plates from the Onyx Service of 1835/36 with reproductions of marble sculptures in the Munich Glyptothek in grisaille on purple-coloured background, including pediment figures from the Aphaia Temple in Aegina, which Thorwaldsen had repaired.

Between the display cases
Four crater-shaped vases; three with tendril decoration and monogram of Max I Joseph; one with gold-engraved grape leaf decoration, about 1820.

Window wall:
Parts of a coffee-service with meander rim 1834/48. - At the sides: Plates with copies from paintings in the Alte Pinakothek, 1820-1825/26.

Narrow wall of the entrance side:
Porcelain pieces from 1842-1845: Plates with scenes from the Nibelungen saga, some of them after Julius Schnorr von Carolsfeld (see Rooms 75-79).

Narrow wall of the exit side:
Porcelain pieces from 1842-1845: Plates with landscapes of the Nibelungen saga. - Plates with female beauties in national cos-

tume. - Plates with Bavarian views, some of them after designs by Domenico Quaglio.

14f Nymphenburg Manufactory - Porcelain pictures

As early as 1810, the then Crown Prince Ludwig of Bavaria placed an order for a table-service with copies of the best paintings in the Munich Royal Gallery. These plates were made by the Nymphenburg Manufactory until 1845 and then once again in 1883, and were put to practical use as scratches on them prove. On the other hand, an extensive series of porcelain plates bearing copies of paintings in the Alte Pinakothek, which King Ludwig I ordered in 1827, were intended solely for documentary purposes: He desired "the copies of the most excellent pictures to be preserved in enamel colours for future generations, when the ravages of time will have finally destroyed the originals."

Christian Adler was one of the most important among the numerous specialists in this complicated and expensive technique. - While many of the services were damaged during World War II, Ludwig I's Gallery of Beauties suffered the greatest losses.

Rightband longitudinal wall:

On the wall: At the left, Max Auer, 1833, after Hans Holbein the Elder (wings of the Sebastian altar), at the right, Christian Adler, 1837, after Albrecht Dürer (The Four Apostles).

In the three display cases (from left to right): Copies from 1827 to 1856 after Italian paintings of the 17th century. - Copies after Italian masters of the 15th/16th century (including Raphael's Madonna Tempi) and German painters of the 16th century (including Dürer's Self-Portrait), masters of Netherlandish painting of the 15th century (including Hans Memling). -

Copies after Italian, Spanish and French painters of the 17th century.

Left longitudinal wall:
On the walls: At the left, Max Legrand 1843, after Francesco Granacci (St. Apollonia and St. Jerome), at the right Christian Adler, 1840, after Raphael's Madonna from the House of Canigiani.
In the three display cases: Copies after Dutch and Flemish masters of the 17th century, including the Crucifixion of Christ by Rembrandt and paintings by Peter Paul Rubens.

Narrow wall of the entrance side:
Plates with copies of paintings from 1811 to 1814. - Detached: Two amphorae with landscapes, first half of the 19th century.

Narrow wall of the exit side:
Plates with copies of paintings from 1810 to 1813, including Crown Prince Ludwig of Bavaria after a painting by Angelica Kauffmann from 1805 to 1807. - Detached: Two crater-shaped vases with landscape pictures in oval frame, about 1820.

14g Berlin Manufactory

On the occasion of the marriage of Crown Prince Maximilian of Bavaria (later King Maximilian II) to the Prussian Princess Marie in 1842, the Berlin court presented the newly-weds with an extensive porcelain service.

Middle display case:
Table-service with floral decoration, before 1842. Figural elements after earlier models. Additional pieces in Nymphenburg porcelain.

Longitudinal wall:
Plates of the table-service with floral decoration, before 1842. - In the five middle display cases (from left to right): Plates with painted backgrounds: Some with views of Fischbach in Silesia, Berlin and unidentified Swiss landscapes; others with hunting scenes, bouquets and copies of paintings, before 1842.

Narrow sides:
Pieces of the table-service with floral decoration, before 1842.

Detached:
Four magnificent amphorae with views of Berlin, about 1840. From left to right: The Altes Museum - The Berlin Palace with the "Long Bridge" - Courtyard view of the Berlin Palace - "Unter den Linden".

THE TOUR RETURNS AND GOES DOWN THE YELLOW STAIRCASE (ROOM 14). FROM THERE IT CONTINUES TO THE ROOMS:

15-21   Rear Electoral Chambers (East Asian Collection)

The suite above the Antiquarium, parallel to the "Front Electoral Chambers", was originally used for the private running of the apartment of Elector Max III Joseph (that is rooms for the servants, auxiliary cabinets, boudoirs, etc.) Since 1920, the collection of East Asian porcelain has been accommodated here, to which the sequence of the so-called Poland Carpets was added in 1966.

THE SO-CALLED POLAND CARPETS
on the walls of the Porcelain Gallery come in part from an art collection which the Wittelsbach acquired as a dowry on the

occasion of the marriage (in 1642) of the daughter of King Sigis-mund III of Poland, Anna Catharina Constanza, with the Philipp Wilhelm (later elector of the Palatinate who died in 1685).

COLLECTION OF EAST ASIAN PORCELAIN
The inventory of the Ducal Art Chamber made by Johann Bap-tist Fickler in 1598 already listed 167 pieces of East Asian porce-lain. From c. 1690, Elector Max Emanuel purchased East Asian porcelainware, most of which he obtained through Holland. He established the "Dutch Cabinet" (1693-1695 laid out in the area of the former Alexander Suites, later incorporated in the recon-struction of the Green Gallery Room 58). Additional East Asian porcelain was added with the Palatinate inheritance under Karl Theodor and Max IV Joseph. Numerous vases, flasks and other vessels as well as figures served (and in some cases still do) as room decoration on mantelpieces and tables or on consoles in cabinets especially installed for them (cf. the Mirror Cabinet of the Rich Rooms, Room 61).

The invention of porcelain in China took place in stages. Prototypes contain-ing kaolin (protoporcelain) are known to have been made during the T'ang dynasty (618-906). By the Sung Dynasty (960-1279), porcelain already existed, even though the ratio of the chemical components (kaolin, feldspar and quartz) still fluctuated. The porcelain compound had already reached a high degree of technical perfection (Imperial Manufactory Chin-tê-chên) when under the Ming Dynasty (1368-1643) export to Europe began. Artistic perfection began in the early years of the Ch'ing (Manchu) Dynasty (1644-1912), and continued in the reign of the Emperor K'ang-hsi (1662-1722). A brief table now follows to permit an easy survey of the dynasties and emperors (after the Nien-Hao periods), for the time during which the porcelain on display was manufactored:

Ming Dynasty	(1368-1643)		
Hsuan-tê	1426-1435	Ch'ia-ching	1522-1566
Chêng-hua	1465-1487	Wan-li	1573-1619
Ch'eng-tê	1506-1521		
Ch'ing (Manchu) Dynasty	(1644-1912)		
K'ang-hsi	1662-1722	Ch'ieng-lung	1736-1795
Yung-chêng	1723-1735		

Japanese porcelain production did not start until the 16th century. According to tradition, the potter Gorodayu go Shonzui learnt the art of porcelain in Ching-tê-chên in China and took it back to his home in Japan. Initially, the raw material was imported from China, until early in the 17th century, when Japanese deposits of kaolin were discovered in Izumi-yama, near Arita (Province Hizen) and exploited. The main export harbour for "Arita" porcelain was the nearby Imari, accounting for the title "Old Imari". Old Imari porcelains took over the cobalt blue under the glaze from Chinese examples. There are additional overglaze colours: Iron red, black and gold. The name of Sakaida Kakiemon, who was active during the first half of the 17th century and whose technique was widely copied, is synonymous with multicolour pure overglaze painting. The later manufactories in Kutani (Kaga Province on Hondo, since c. 1640) were unable to sell the bulk of their products in Europe until the 19th century.

15 First Room of the East Asian Collection

Near Eastern carpets, most of them belonging to the group of so-called Poland Carpets

On the window piers (starting from the left):
Woven carpet with ornamental pattern.
Kaschan (Persia), early 17th century.

Oriental brocade table-cloth; pattern: Tendrils and birds.
Embroidery in appliqué technique in gold, silver and coloured silk threads on linen base. Persia, probably 18th century.

Knotted carpet with ornamental pattern.
Knotting technique with Souma effects in gold and silver threads. Persia, 17th century.

Woven carpet with Polish armorial eagle of King Sigismund III.
Kaschan (Persia), 1601, delivered to Poland in 1602 for Sigismund III.

Knotted carpet with depiction of animals in combat.
Knotting technique with Souma effects in gold and silver threads. Persia, 17th century.

On the rear wall, between the display cases (to the rear):
Knotted carpet with blue tendril ornamentation.
Probably Isfahan or Kaschan (Persia). first quarter of the 17th century (heavily worn).

Knotted carpet with small-part tendril ornament.
Probably Isfahan or Kaschan (Persia). first quarter of 17th century (heavily worn).

Chinese porcelain

At the side of the entrance:
Two vases in baluster form (large long-necked flasks); colours of the so-called "famille verte", K'ang-hsi Era.

In the first group of display cases: *Fig. 27*
Mostly products in the colours of the so-called "famille verte" (Wan-li-wu-ts'ai), approximately 17th and early 18th century.
Green shades (copper green) in combination with iron red and black are preferred. Frequent appearance of this colour scheme in the K'ang-hsi Era (1662-1722).
The figural pieces placed in between them are in the technique of the "Email sur biscuit", mostly in French bronze fire-gilded mounts.

Opposite on the window pier:
Three-piece vase set of the "famille verte" with luxurious landscape and floral decoration.

In the second group of display cases:
Blueware (underglaze blue), c. 16th to 18th century.

This type of glaze used frequently from the Ming Era uses the blue of cobalt oxide under the glaze. Imports from the Near East bring the best colour to China, the "Mohammedan Blue" (hui-hui-ch'ing). Occasionally additional overglaze decoration is seen (in iron red, green and gold).

Of particular interest (5th middle display case, middle shelf): Calyx bowl; in the central pictorial section: Nightingale; outside: Picture scrolls, tables with bowls, books with strap ornaments and tassels (Wan-li Era); gilded silver mounts, probably South German about 1590-1600, as well as (top, middle) an additional bowl with various images on the outsides: The three-clawed dragon (good luck symbol); on the bottom good wishes: Ch'ang ming fu kuei, meaning long life, wealth, honour (Wan-li Era); gilded silver mounts, probably South German about 1590-1600 (both probably from the Art Chamber of Duke Albrecht V, prior to 1598).

On both sides of the group of display cases and opposite on the window pier:
Sets of monumental vases with blue underglaze.

In the third group of display cases:
Predominantly items with colours of the so-called "famille rose", dating to around the late 17th and 18th century.

This colour scheme comes from the addition of white and aims to achieve pastel effects. It is based on a European invention of the 17th century and is therefore called "Yang-ts'ai", foreign colours. The majority of this sort of porcelain was made in the 18th century, in the period of Emperor Yung-chêng (1723-1735) and Ch'ien-lung (1736-1795).

Also: Figural pieces in the "Email sur biscuit" technique as well as "Celadon ware" with grey-green glaze (so called after the shepherd attired in grey-green of the novel "L'Astrée" by Hon-oré d'Urfé) and crackleware. Several pieces with French bronze or silver mounts.

Opposite on the window pier:
Three-piece vase set in colours of the "famille rose", decorated

with a pond with lotus plants and fish, above birds and insects (Yung-chêng Era).

At the left of the exit:
Large vase with peony decoration in the "famille verte" colour-scheme (probably K'ang-hsi Era).

16 Second Room of the East Asian Collection

On the window side:
Two cylindrical pots, originally garden stools. Imitation of older "Celadon Porcelain" probably from the early Ming Dynasty (probably K'ang-hsi Era); gilt bronze mounts with a copper liner probably Paris c. 1710-1720.

Display case in front of the rear wall:
Large Fo-dog group, "Email sur biscuit" (K'ang-hsi Era), indi-vidual parts in the base are Japanese.
The Fo-dog is leaning on the brocade or silk ball, an old Buddhistic treasure, the bitch is playing with her puppies. - Clock crown: Pu-tai, the merry mendi-cant monk (Bodhisattva Maitraya), so-called Blanc-de-Chine porcelain of the Têhua Manufactory, Fukien Province, with overglaze colours in iron red, green and black. The gilt bronze mounts of the mantelpiece clock and the table can-delabra (branches removed): Paris, towards the middle of the 18th century. Clockwork by Pierre Le Roy, Société des arts.

17 Third Room of the East Asian Collection

Group of display cases at the left:
So-called Blanc-de-Chine porcelain of the Tê-hua Manufac-tory, Fukien Province, mostly of the 17th and 18th century.
Characteristic: The fine surface glaze, milky white to cream coloured. Figural depictions are preferred. - The objects probably all belong to the K'ang-hsi Era. - Including French silver and bronze mounts.

In the detached display case opposite:
Three-part black vase set (mirror black); K'ang-hsi Era. Gold decoration on the black glaze: Decorative friezes, as well as Fo-dogs, fabulous creatures, fish, birds, flowers, plum branches and poems.

18 Former Cecilia Chapel (Fourth Room of the East Asian Collection)

The small centralized room with high ceiling and wall niches into which you can see from Room 17 was started in 1693 at the order of Elector Max Emanuel to designs by the architect Henrico Zuccalli. The decoration started in 1704 with further work done on the chapel in 1715. The room was damaged in the Residence fire of 1729; new decoration about 1756. Consecration in 1757. The appointments of the chapel were (with the exception of several portable pieces) destroyed in World War II. The skeletal structure along with the flat dome and the high wall niches survived. In 1966, the room was obtained for the East Asian Collection and set up as a Porcelain Cabinet; analogously to the so-called "Dutch Cabinet" (the title refers to Holland as main trading place for East Asian porcelainware) which originally was immediately adjacent; it was built from 1693 to 1695, and later gave way for the construction of the Green Gallery (Room 58).

Particular attention is drawn to the following pieces of porcelain:
Above, all around: Dishes and plates from an extensive set with the coat of arms of a Palatinate-Hessian alliance, allegedly Palatine-Sulzbach with Hesse-Rheinfels-Rothenburg, in the colours of the "famille rose" (perhaps late K'ang-hsi Era, compare plates of the same set in Room 15, 9th display case below). In the niches of the entrance and transverse axis: Kuan-yin fig-

ures, so-called Blanc-de-Chine of the Tê-hua Manufactory, including one with (probably) European cold painting (probably K'ang-hsi Era). All three in the middle of Japanese plates (striking here because of the dark cobalt blue) with floral decoration; depiction in the middle: Cranes (Old Imari).

Chandelier, German(?), c. 1800.

19 Fifth Room of the East Asian Collection

Group of display cases at the left:
Blueware with overglaze decoration, here 17th and 18th century. Above the blue underglaze (cf. Room 15, second group of china cabinets) are iron red and gold overglaze colours, sometimes also copper green and other colours. Within this type of painted porcelain, is a distinct class known as Chinese Imari which is characterised by the blue-red-gold (and sometimes also black) colour combination. It adopts from Japanese Imari ware the dense surface decoration as well as certain decorative themes (for this compare the Japanese "Old Imari" in the opposite display case). - A special group of objects has a restricted, but striking, palette of iron red and gold over a white glaze. - All pieces belong to the K'ang-hsi or Yung-chêng Dynasty.

Above the group of display cases:
Plates of the so-called Chinese Imari type.

Group of display cases at the right:
Japanese porcelain, 17th and 18th century (cf. p. 39).
Arita ware, so-called Old Imari: Characteristic is the colour combination of a cobalt blue under-glaze with iron red, black

and gold, as well as the intensity of the painting, most of whose motives come from brocade weaving.

The Kaiemon painting type, named after Sakaida Kakiemon (active in the first half of the 17th century) prefers light, powerful shades above the milky white glaze. The surface decorated but with large areas left bare.

Above the group of display cases and on both sides:
Plates and vases of the Japanese Old Imari type.

20 Sixth Room of the East Asian Collection

Furnishings:
Lacquered cabinet, Japan, early years of the 18th century.

Landscape scenes in gold sequins technique (Nashi-ji); on the interior: Cranes at a pond edge. Continuous chessboard frieze with mother-of-pearl lamina. Engraved and gilded metal mounts.

Ten-piece folding screen, so-called Coromandel lacquer, China, about 1700.

This lacquer technique takes its name from its transshipment ports on the Coromandel Coast on the south-east of the Indian Peninsula. However this folding screen is Chinese work (here probably of the K'ang-hsi Era).

Vase with lid, Japan, late 17th/early 18th century.

Group of display cases on the rear wall:
Japanese porcelain, 17th and 18th century.

Of particular interest:

Lower left: Large plate in the Old Imari painting style, blue underglaze and gold. Depiction: Cranes, floral decoration on the rim. - Two vessels in shell form with Celadon glaze after a Chinese model (perhaps Okawachi or Nabeshima porcelain).

Middle left: Reclining elephant and two boys; mounts of the mantelpiece clock probably Paris towards the middle of the 18th century; clock case and crown likewise of Japanese porcelain. - Two bowls with lids with primarily red painting (on the lid modelled tree stump with blossoms); decoration in the panels, in the Kakiemon style.

Above: Large plate, predominantly red. Depiction: Ladies with ladles and food bowls, dancing around a large vessel decorated with a dragon.

Middle right: Elephant; gilt bronze mounts as mantelpiece clock, Paris c. 1720, clockwork by Etienne Lenoir. - Box with insert (cricket cage), walls in honeycomb pattern.

Above: Large plate, primarily red. Panels in the shape of picture rolls. At the left, a lady playing the flute with two accompanists, at the right man with soap bubbles in the midst of a swarm of children; in other panels, landscapes; at the top fanciful bird.

Above the group of display cases:
Set of Vases, coated with black lacquer with coloured painting, Japan, 18th century.

21 Seventh Room of the East Asian Collection

On the walls
At the right: Painted Chinese silk wall covering, 18th century. Middle: Woven carpet, Kaschan (Persia), first half of the 17th century (belonging to the series of the so-called Poland carpets).
At the left: Tribunal rug, made in patchwork style, Near East (Damascus?), 17th or 18th century.

On the floor:
Patchwork knotted carpet, probably Near East, 17th or 18th century.

Two fish vessels and two large vases with lids, China, 18th century (Ch'ieng-lung?, "famille rose").

Glass chandeliers, German, middle of the 18th century.

22-31 Electoral Chambers

From its erection in 1569 until about 1599, the upper floor above the Antiquarium functioned as the Ducal Library. During the 17th and early part of the 18th century, the apartment of the hereditary prince was located in this area. - After the death of Emperor Karl VII (1745), whose private apartment was the so-called "Yellow Suite" (today Porcelain Chambers of the 18th century, Room 82-88) Elector Max III Joseph and his wife Maria Anna maintained the apartment of the hereditary prince. The suite was appointed under the supervision of Johann Baptist Gunetzrhainer in 1746 to 1748: Antechamber, audience or conference room, state bedroom, and cabinet - in the northwest part for the elector and in reverse order in the adjoining south-east part for the electress. In 1760-1763, the appointments were embellished and in some cases replaced under the supervision of François Cuvilliés the Elder. - These rooms were destroyed during World War II. They were restored, at least in their essential features, with the moveable works of art which were largely preserved and from remnants of the panelling.

The visitor now crosses through the two following Rooms 24 and 23, in order to start the circular tour through the Electoral Chambers from Room 22 in reverse order, but in correct sequence.

22 Antechamber (Small Knights' Room)

Wainscotted room with sparse carving, painted green from 1763.
Additions in 1960-1965: Wainscot, smooth parts of the panelling.

Overdoor
Joseph Stephan: Four ideal landscapes, 1765.

Probably Franz Joseph Winter: Elector Max III Joseph (reigned from 1745 to 1777) and his wife Maria Anna Sophie (daughter of King August III of Poland, Elector of Saxony) in hunting costume, about 1750.

Georg Anton Abraham Urlaub: Countess Maria Josepha von Paumgarten-Frauenstein, 1782.
Pastel. It was Countess Paumgarten who arranged for Wolfgang Amadeus Mozart to obtain a commission from Elector Karl Theodor to write the opera Idomeneo, which was premiered in Munich in 1781. On 30 September 1777 Mozart asked in this room the then Elector Max III Joseph for a position at court, but was turned down with the often-quoted words, "There is no vacancy available".

Furnishings
Faience stove, South German c. 1770.

Two commodes, Munich(?), middle of the 18th century.
Oak, walnut and other woods; gilt bronze appliqués.

Six taborets, Munich about 1740.
Carved, painted gold and white, coverings replaced.

Glass chandelier, probably South German, middle of the 18th century.

23 Antechamber (Dining Room)

Before 1944, the room had a framed wainscot of the 19th century. A new restrained wall covering has taken its place. Richly carved and gilded overdoor frames of 1765.

Overdoors
Joseph Stephan: View of Markt Schwaben (above the entrance

door) and view of Dachau (above the exit door), both from 1765.

Paintings on the walls

Bernardo Bellotto, named Canaletto (1721-1780), 1761: Munich from the East (on the rear wall) *(Fig. 31)*.

Nymphenburg Palace from the Park Side (right sidewall).

Nymphenburg Palace from the City Side (left sidewall).

The vedutas are part of the original decoration of the dining room after the redesign of the suite of rooms by François Cuvilliés the Elder in 1760-1763. They were already mentioned in an inventory of 1767 as part of the decorations of this room.

Furnishings

Faience stove, Danube area (Vienna?) about 1760-1770.

Three commodes (semi cabinets), Munich about 1746/50.

By Johann Michael or Johann Adam Schmidt, spruce and limewood with flat carving in rocaille shapes, gilded, on white base. Marble tops replaced. - On top of them:

Vase with lid, porcelain, China, 18th century.

At the left: Mantelpiece clock, Paris about 1780.

Group: Mercury instructs a girl in the art of love. Gilt bronze on alabaster base, clockwork signed by Imbert l'ainé (Jean-Gabriel Imbert).

At the right: Mantelpiece clock, Paris about 1750/60.

Gilt bronze, partially with cold enamel. Clockwork by Louis Montjoye, Paris. Bronze mounts Paris. Porcelain group: Meissen Manufactory. Porcelain flowers: Chantilly Manufactory.

Four chairs, Munich about 1760.

Carved, painted white and gold. Coverings replaced.

Longcase clock on wall bracket, France about 1750.

Clockwork by Joseph Krapp, Munich, c. 1780/90. - The portrait medallion inserted at that time shows the Elector Karl Theodor.

Four sconces, Munich about 1760.

Probably by Benedikt Hässler. Carved and gilded rocaille frames, in them flat candlestick mirror with cut glass. Two-piece candle branches in gilt bronze. (Two additional ones in Room 31).

Glass chandelier, probably Irish, 18th century.

24 Audience Chamber of the Elector

The second remodelling of this suite about 1760-1763 brought the wall panellings and mirrors as well as the stucco work (probably by Franz Xaver Feuchtmayer).

The paintings and their frames, the overdoor frames of the door openings in the enfilade and the carved sconces remain from the old appointments. Doors and window shutters come from an earlier context (Effner period, c. 1720-1730). Both the panelling and the stucco work was made in 1960-1965 after the original designs.

Overdoors

Johann Heinrich Roos: Two ideal landscapes (over the doors of the enfilade).

School of Franz Joachim Beich: Ideal landscape (rear wall at the left).

School of Johann Anton Eismann: Night scene with Fishermen (rear wall at the right).

Painting in the middle of the rear wall

School of George Desmarées: Elector Max III Joseph, towards 1750.

Paintings on the sidewalls

Joachim von Sandrart (attribution): The Twelve Months, about 1650.

Furnishings

Two console tables, Munich about 1760.
Limewood, white, with gilded low relief carving. - On top of them:

Equestrian statuette of Elector Max III Joseph, Charles Dubut the Younger(?), about 1760.
Polychromed wax.

Cylindrical vase, Chinese porcelain, 18th century.
Colours of the "famille rose", Yung-chêng or Ch'ien-lung Dynasty.

Eight taborets, Munich about 1760.
Limewood, white with gilded ornaments. Coverings: Woven fabric from the Munich Gobelin Manufactory c. 1760.

Twelve sconces, Munich about 1760-1763.
Limewood, carved and gilded.

Chandelier, probably South German, middle of the 18th century.

25 Bedroom of the Elector

The room was provided with richly carved and stuccoed decoration after 1760 which was destroyed in 1944. The panelling and the mantelpiece mirror on the window pier come from another context. Of the old appointments, there remain the overdoors and their frames above the enfilade doors. The two rear overdoor frames are copies. The essential pieces of the mobile furnishings are original.

Hanging on the rear wall
Coloured appliqué embroidery on silk, Munich 1748-1786, on which the Electress Maria Anna worked.
The appliqué embroidery of the rear wall and that around the side walls comes from the Bavarian Cabinet of the Koblenz Palace, Residence of the Elector of Treves Clemens Wenzeslaus of Saxony, the brother of Maria Anna (see page 86).

Hanging of the side walls
Raw silk (replaced) with braiding in coloured appliqué embroidery, Munich 1784-1786.

Mantelpiece mirror frame on the window pier
Munich c. 1720/1730.

Overdoors
Johann Michael Rottmayr (attributed): Healing of the Blindman and the Good Samaritan, Munich c. 1700 (in the enfilade).

Style of Giambattista Pittoni: Abraham blesses Isaac and Sacrifice of Isaac, Venice, middle of the 18th century (at the rear).

Paintings on the walls
George Desmarées: Elector Max III Joseph and Ferdinand Count of Salern (Court Theatre Manager 1749-1753), signed and dated 1755 *(Fig. 25)*.

Johann Nikolaus de Grooth: Small Court Concert of the Elector Max III Joseph (with his wife Maria Anna and his sister Maria Antonia, Electress of Saxony), 1758.

Furnishings
State bed. Embroidery of the sole surviving canopy by Franz Joseph Antoni Janssens, Munich about 1757.
Silver lamé with silver embroidery and green velvet with gold embroidery.

Bed drapery c. 1760/70.
Coloured chenille embroidery applied on satin.

Two console tables (at the sides of the bed), Munich about 1730-1740.
Limewood, carved and gilded. - On top of them:

Two candelabra pyramids, probably Munich about 1730-1740.
Crystal. Gilt bronze.

Two commodes, Johann Thomas Sailler, Munich 1761.
Limewood, gilded carving on white background. Gilt bronze fittings. Marble tops replaced. - On top of them:

Two vases with lid with chinoiseries in Hoeroldt painting, Meissen (AR mark) c. 1730.

Four armchairs, Munich about 1760.
Limewood. Carved and gilded on white ground. The chenille embroidery (1760-1770), matching the bed drapery, is applied on satin.

Four sconces, probably Johann Tobias Grün, Munich c. 1760/65.
Limewood, carved and gilded. Large rocaille cartouches each with two carved candle branches. (Two further sconces of this series are in Room 31).

Glass chandelier, probably South German, 18th century.

26 Blue Cabinet (former Library Room)

Powder cabinet before 1762, then library room, later furnished as a kind of cabinet for miniatures.
The carved overdoor frames and the paintings come from the period of 1762-1763. The stove was added in about 1780. Wall hanging replaced (from old designs).

Overdoors

Johann Jakob Dorner the Elder: Two market scenes, probably late 18th century.

Miniatures
Entrance wall, upper row (from right to left)

German, 18th century: Oriental Woman. Belongs to a series of four miniature pictures on parchment "painted in such a manner as if each were attached to a board" (Catalogue 1770), i.e. in Trompe l'oeil manner (tempera).

Maximilian de Geer: Siege (dated 1754) and two cavalry battles (water-colour and tempera).

German, 18th century: Oriental man (counterpart, see above).

Lower row

Dutch, 17th century: Church Interior (oil/copper), according to the 1770 catalogue "by Frank".

German, middle of the 18th century: Battle Scene (gouache).

Maximilian de Geer: Two cavalry battles, c. 1750-1760 (water-colour and tempera).

German, middle of the 18th century: Battle Scene (gouache).

Dutch, 17th century: Church Interior (oil/copper, see above for counterpart).

Rear wall on both sides of the stove

Joseph Weiss: Esther before Ahasuerus and Salomon sacrifices to the Gods, both signed and dated 1767 (water-colour and tempera).

Exit wall, upper row (from left to right)

German, 18th century: Old Woman with Head Scarf (for the style of the depiction, see the Oriental couple opposite).

Maximilian de Geer: View of the Badenburg in the Nymphenburg Palace Park, c. 1730 (water-colour and tempera).

Joseph Werner: Anchises appearing to Aeneas, c. 1676/77 (water-colour and tempera).

Maximilian de Geer: View of the Pagodenburg in the Nymphenburg Palace Park, c. 1730 (water-colour and tempera).

German, 18th century: Old Man (see above for the counterpart).

Middle row

German (Augsburg?), early 17th century: Moses Striking Water from the Rock and Sermon of John the Baptist (oil and tempera on heliotrope utilizing the stone structure).

Lower row

C. Scharner: St. Mary Magdalene (oil/wood), signed "CS(?) fecit 1680".

Joseph Werner: Unknown Young Prince as Cupid (water-colour and tempera), signed and dated 1668, at the bottom the inscription: Nec fraeno nec viribus opus.

F. Matheus Schaeffler: Elector Karl Albrecht dedicates himself to the "Beautiful Maria" of Wessobrunn (water-colour on parchment), signed, c. 1730.

Maximilian de Geer: Landshut with Burg Trausnitz, after the painting of Franz Joachim Beich in the gallery of Nymphenburg Palace, c. 1730 (water-colour and tempera).

Amalie Pachelbel: Floral Piece (oil/wood), purchased by "His Electoral Serene Highness in 1760" according to the 1770 catalogue.

Furnishings

Faience stove, Munich about 1780.

Desk, Abraham and David Roentgen, Neuwied 1773.

Maple, frame maple, rosewood and variously coloured woods, bronze appliqués. Dated by inscription: "Almanach 1773" - On top:

Small candelabrum, Paris c. 1780, in the style of Pierre Gouthière.

Dancing putto with tambourine. Bronze, part gilded, alabaster base.

Small table, Jakob Kieser, Mannheim, soon after 1763.

Rosewood, kingwood, amaranth, boxwood, lemonwood, walnut, maple.

Rotary chair, Georges Jacob, Paris 1781/82.

From the "Cabinet de Conseil" from Karlsberg Castle. Walnut, carved and gilded. Covering renewed. With monogram of Duchess Maria Amalia of Palatine-Zweibrücken.

Four corner chairs, France c. 1780, reworked in the second half of the 19th century.

Beechwood, carved and gilded, covering replaced.

Fireplace screen, Munich 1766.
Limewood, carved and gilded, with woven fabric of the Munich Gobelin Manufactory, signed "Klein 1766" (Joseph Klein).

Two sconces, Paris c. 1700.
Gilt bronze.

Chandelier, middle of the 18th century.

27 Yellow Cabinet (Writing Room)

Originally (1762) tea cabinet.
Toward 1800s, the room was given new wall hangings, and its current one in 1965.

Overdoors
Peter Jakob Horemans: Two Floral Still Lifes, signed and dated 1768.

Painting on the rear wall
Joseph Lander: Elector Max III Joseph (pastel), 1766, signed and dated on the back.

Paintings and miniatures on the entrance wall
Christian Seybold: Old Woman and Old Man, c. 1750 (oil/wood).
Joseph Adam Moelckh: St. Joseph as Intercessor, c. 1750/51 (oil/copper).
In between and below: Seven scenes from the Soldier's Life after Jacques Callot ("Grandes misères de la guerre", 1630), probably German, second half of the 17th century (oil/wood).

Paintings and miniatures on the exit wall
F.C. Tecler: Two River Landscapes, 18th century (oil/wood).
Joseph Adam Moelckh: Beheading of a Saint (Paul?), c. 1750/51 (oil/copper).
In between and below: Seven scenes from the Soldier's Life after Callot, probably German, second half of the 17th century (as above).

Furnishings

Secretary, Jean-François Oeben, Paris about 1754/56 *(Fig. 32)*.
Veneer of rosewood, satin rosewood and amaranth with rich flower marquetry
of coloured woods. Gilt bronze fittings, perhaps by Claude-Thomas Duplessis.
Marble top replaced.

Commode, attributed to Jean-Pierre Latz, Paris about 1753/54.
Veneer of rosewood, satin rosewood and amaranth with rich flower marquetry
of coloured woods. Gilt bronze fittings. Marble top replaced. - On top:

Mantelpiece clock, Paris about 1780, with the group of Hebe
and Cupid.
Gilt bronze, alabaster. Clockwork signed Henri Voisin, Paris.

Combined desk and vanity table, Jean-François Oeben, Paris
about 1754/57.
Veneer of rosewood, satin rosewood and amaranth with rich flower marquetry
of coloured woods. Gilt bronze fittings.

Sewing table, Jean-François Oeben, Paris about 1755.
Veneer of kingwood, rosewood, satin rosewood and amaranth, top with flower
marquetry of coloured wood. Gilt bronze fittings.

Four lounge chairs, after designs by Jean-Démosthène
Dugourc, Paris about 1785.
The chairs come from the mirror cabinet of the former palace of King Max I.
Joseph, the Hôtel des Deux-Ponts in Strassburg. Walnut, beech, carved,
painted white and part gilded. Covers renewed.

Fireplace screen, Georges Jacob, Paris about 1780/82.
Beech, lime, carved and gilded. Coverings with pheasant motifs: Brocaded silk
lampas, after designs by Philippe de Lasalle, Pernon Manufactory, Lyon. (See
the fireplace screen in Room 37).

Two sconces, Paris about 1780.
Gilt bronze.

Chandelier, middle of the 18th century.

28 Former Bedroom of the Electress

The remodelling in 1762 converted this room into a bedroom for the Electress. After the war damage of 1944, too little remained to permit a restoration of the original bedroom (in red damask). Wall hangings replaced.

Overdoors
School of Giovanni Francesco Barbieri, named Guercino(?): Cimon and Pera, Rebecca and Eleazar at the Well.

Tapestries
Four woven tapestries from the Hunting Series, made by the Beauvais Manufactory under the direction of Noël-Antoine de Merou, after designs by Jean-Baptiste Oudry, about 1727.
From right to left: Boar hunt, badger baiting, stag hunt, wolf hunt.

Furnishings
Two commodes, Charles Cressent, Paris about 1730/35.
Rosewood with inlays, bronze fittings, marble top (replaced).

Commode, attributed to Pierre Roussel, Paris about 1755.
The commode bears the stamp of the dealer and ebony specialist Denis Genty. Veneer of kingwood and rosewood with strap-work in amaranth. Gilt bronze fittings. Marble top by Brèche d'Alep. - On the three commodes:

Three pot-pourris (vessels for holding perfume), Japanese porcelain, so-called Old Imari, late 17th/early 18th century.
Baluster-shaped, with honeycomb pattern.

Two chandeliers, late 18th century.
Alabaster and gilt bronze.

Two encoignures (corner cabinets), Bernhard II Vanrisamburgh, signed, Paris about 1740.

Rosewood veneer with inlays in kingwood. Gilt bronze fittings. Marble top replaced. - On top:

Two girandoles, Paris about 1780.
Gilt bronze and alabaster.

Longcase clock, Munich about 1760/70.
Walnut with checkered marquetry. On the corner attached arches and scrolls, carved. - Clock case probably by Georg Sebastian Guglhör, clockwork by Christian Nitsche.

Four armchairs, German, middle of the 18th century.
Limewood, carved and gilded. Coverings replaced.

Six sconces, Paris about 1725.
Gilt bronze.

Chandelier, about 1760.
Perhaps after the turned model of Cardinal Johann Theodor of Bavaria. Gilt bronze.

29 Audience Chamber of the Electress

The old appointments of 1746-1748 and 1760-1763 were destroyed in 1944, as was the famed stove of 1763 in cabinet form and its counterpart. The marble mantelpiece comes from the late 18th century. Wall hangings replaced.

Overdoors
Two Still Lives by Christoffel Puytlinck, c. 1700.
Two Still Lives, 17th/18th century.

Tapestries
Two woven hangings from the Hunting Series of the Beauvais

Manufactory under the management of Noël-Antoine de Merou after designs by Jean-Baptiste Oudry, around 1727.
At the right Fox Hunt, at the left Roebuck Hunt.

Two framed woven portraits
Elector Max III Joseph and his wife Maria Anna, after designs by George Desmarées woven in the Munich Gobelin Manufactory, signed and dated: Chédeville 1777.

Furnishings
Throne canopy, probably Munich, towards the middle of the 18th century.
Appliqué embroidery on green damask. Hangings replaced.

Two console tables, probably by Johann Caspar Hörspurcher, Munich about 1755.
Limewood, carved and gilded. Marble top replaced. - On top:

Mantelpiece clock with Aurora waking Cupid; Paris about 1780.
Gilt bronze, alabaster. Clockwork by Imbert l'aîné, Paris (Jean-Gabriel Imbert). From the Zweibrücken Palace in Strasbourg.

Porcelain vase, Japan, so-called Old-Imari, late 17th early 18th century.

Throne-chair, Munich about 1750.
Limewood, carved and gilded. Original covering: Red silk velvet with appliquéd silver braiding.

Four armchairs and two taborets, Munich about 1730.
Limewood, carved, painted white and gold. Covering replaced.

Two guéridons, Munich about 1730.
Limewood, carved and gilded. Intarsia on the upper surface.

Knotted carpet on the throne step: Persia, early 17th century.
Part of the group of the "Poland Carpets": See Room 15.

Four sconces (two different pairs), Paris about 1740.
Gilt bronze.

Mirror on window pier, German (Lohr), first half of the 18th century.

Chandelier, probably German, middle of the 18th century.

30 Antechamber

The formerly simple panelling (19th century) was destroyed in 1944. The furnishings are preserved.

Overdoors

Four still lifes of fruit and flowers, Franz Werner Tamm, about 1700.

Tapestries

Three woven hangings from the "Great Mogul Series", produced in the Beauvais Manufactory, probably under the supervision of Noël-Antoine de Merou, from designs by Jean-Baptiste Blin de Fontenay, Guy-Louis Vernansal the Elder, and Jean-Baptiste Monnoyer, about 1730.
Depictions (from right to left): The Astronomers *(Fig. 26)*, The Audience, The Banquet.

Furnishings

Two commodes, Paris about 1745.
Kingwood veneer. Gilt bronze fittings. One marble top replaced, one of Tegernsee marble. - On top:

Two candelabra with putti (at the right), probably Antoine-André Ravrio, Paris about 1810.
Bronze, part gilded.

Two candelabra with boy and girl (at the left), Vienna (?), early 19th century.
Bronze, part gilded.

Bureau plat (Desk), German 18th century.
Black stained wood. Gilt bronze fittings. Leather covering replaced.

Desk chair, probably South German about 1750.
Carved and gilded, covering replaced.

Candlestick, Paris about 1740, in the style of Juste-Aurèle Meissonier.
Gilt bronze.

Four taborets, Munich about 1740.
Carved, painted white and gold.

Long-case clock, case probably Rhenish (Düsseldorf?), first half of the 18th century.
Walnut, veneered, frame straps of plumwood. Gildings. Clockwork: London, with calendar, lunar cycle and striking mechanism.

Two sconces (on the rear wall) with Harlequin and Pierrot, Paris about 1725.
Gilt bronze.

Four sconces (on the side walls) with the figures of America and Asia, Paris about 1725, in the style of André-Charles Boulle.
Gilt bronze.

Chandelier, Abraham II Drentwett, Augsburg about 1708-1716.
Rich silver embossing, part gilded. Under the crowning electoral hat three cartouche panels with coats of arms of the Palatine Electorate, of the Medici and
monogram of the Elector Johann Wilhelm (reigned from 1690 to 1716, married to Anna Maria Luisa of Tuscany). In between (cast) putti with the chain
of the Order of the Golden Fleece and of the Knights of St. Hubert.

31 Cloakroom

Stove, Munich about 1750.
Restored from fragments.

Tapestry

Hanging from the "Great Mogul Series", Beauvais Manufac-
tory, probably under the supervision of Noël-Antoine de
Merou, about 1730.
Pineapple Harvest. See Room 30.

Furnishings

Two commodes, Matthieu Criaerd, signed, Paris about 1740.
Kingwood veneer. Gilt bronze appliqués. One French and one Tegernsee marble top.

Wall clock, Paris about 1750.
Gilt bronze. Rocaille forms. Clockwork by Jean-Baptiste Baillon, Paris (signed
on the inside).

Four sconces, Munich about 1760/65.
Limewood, carved and gilded (cf. Room 25), two with flat candlestick mirrors
and gilt bronze branches (cf. Room 23).

Chandelier, probably German, second half of the 18th century.

Proceed through the Black Hall (Room 13) then into the All
Saints' Corridor (Room 32).

32 All Saints' Corridor

The connecting passageway between the Black Hall and the former Apothecary Block (which today houses the Old Residence Theatre) corresponds in the first six axes to the wings of the south side of the Fountain Courtyard. Formerly, its east end also connected with the upper storey of the All Saints' Court Church by Klenze. After the junction with the so-called Charlotte Wing (north-eastern wing of the Fountain Courtyard), this corridor belongs to the 19th century (Klenze about 1830). The ceiling stuccowork, mostly replaced, corresponds stylistically to this construction period.

Series of Italian landscape pictures, Munich 1830/33, by Carl Rottmann.

Since 1966, the All Saints' Corridor has contained the fresco cycle of Italian landscapes, which Carl Rottmann painted in 1830-1833 for King Ludwig I as decorations for the west wing of the Court Garden Arcades. Klenze had redesigned the arcades at that time and suggested to the king that it be decorated with frescoes. The Italian cycle could be seen in the Court Garden Arcades until 1943. The frescos were then removed during World War II under extremely difficult conditions and stored in safety.

The intention of the cycle is an "Italian trip in pictures". - It was possible to maintain the original sequence as in the Court Garden Arcades when the pictures were accommodated in the All Saints' Corridor after the war. While Klenze's frame decorations had to be omitted, the poems pertaining to the landscapes composed by King Ludwig I were included.

33-37   So-called Court Garden Rooms

The north-eastern wing of the Fountain Courtyard contained a long corridor in the early 17th century, which was divided into small rooms with gilded wooden coffered ceilings c. 1616-1615 (see the painting in Room 50). The wing is now called the "Charlotte Wing" after the former apartment appointed around

1814 for Princess Charlotte Auguste (daughter of King Max I Joseph). The rooms 39-41 recall this period. In 1966, parts of the Court Garden Rooms were inserted into the remaining rooms.

The contents of the following five so-called Court Garden Rooms come for the most part from Karlsberg Castle near Homburg (in the vicinity of Zweibrücken). This palace, named after its builder, Duke Karl II August of Palatine-Zweibrücken, was built from 1776 by Johann Christian Mannlich and furnished under his supervision by important French artists. The Revolutionary Army burnt down this palace complex in a few days - at that time one of the largest palaces of the 18th century. The brother of Karl August, Max IV Joseph, brought what could be rescued of the movable works of art to Munich when he assumed the vacant electoral dignity upon the death of Karl Theodor. In 1799/1800, the rescued appointments were integrated first into the old apartments of the Residence.

At the same time Max IV. Joseph ordered the installation of a state apartment for the Electress Caroline in the northern part of the Munich Residence. Since these rooms faced the Court Garden, they received the name "Court Garden Rooms". The rooms were first designed and fitted under the direction of Charles-Pierre Puille from 1799-1804, then by Andreas Gärtner c. 1809. The furniture was renewed in classical style.

On the occasion of the engagement of King Ludwig II with Duchess Sophie in Bayern in 1867 the court garden rooms were redesigned in the Louis XVI style and refurnished with furniture from Karlsberg Castle.

The Court Garden Rooms were gutted in 1944. Since it was possible to restore the Imperial Hall, which had originally been located here, the works of art were newly assembled in 1966 in some rooms of the "Charlotte Wing" on the Fountain Courtyard (Rooms 33-38).

33 First so-called Court Garden Room

Tapestry

From a series about Rinaldo and Armida, the Gobelin Manufactory Paris, Jacques Neilson, after designs by Charles Coypel,
after 1762.
Scene from the opera "Rinaldo and Armida" by Philippe Quinault: Rinaldo's
Sleep. The series comes from the Parisian Palais Deux-Ponts of Duke Christian IV of Palatine-Zweibrücken.

Paintings

Moritz von Kellerhoven: Maria Leopoldine of Austria, second
wife of Elector Karl Theodor, about 1795.

South German: Elector Karl Theodor, before 1787 (part copy
after Pompeo Batoni 1775).

Furnishings

Console table, Munich about 1800.
Copy of the console tables of François-Joseph Duret in Room 36. Beech, limewood, carved and gilded. Marble top replaced. Gilding probably renewed c.
1867 by the company Franz Radspieler in Munich. - On top:

Two bronze urns on alabaster bases, towards 1800.
Bronze, part gilded.

Two commodes, French, about 1780.
Veneer of rosewood and palisander with marquetry in boxwood and bog oak
and amaranth banding. Gilt bronze fittings, marble top (replaced). - On top:

Two pairs of candlesticks, possibly Vienna about 1810
(entrance side) and Paris about 1810 (exit side).
Gilt bronze.

Chiffonnière (sewing table) with straight legs, Jean-Pierre
Dusautoy, signed, Paris about 1770/75.

Chiffonnière (sewing table) with straight legs, attributed to Jean-Pierre Dusautoy, Paris about 1775/80.

Marquetry of natural-coloured and stained box, amaranth and maple in rosewood veneer. Bronze and brass fittings. White marble tops.

Sofa and four armchairs from a 14-piece suite, Paris about 1770/75.

Beechwood, carved and gilded. Woven coverings with motifs after François Boucher and Jean-Baptiste Oudry, Jacques Neilson, Gobelin Manufactory, Paris.

Wall clock with crowning vase (on the window pier), Paris about 1770.

Gilt bronze. Clockwork by Royer, Paris.

Two sconces, Paris about 1770, in the style of Jean-Charles Delafosse.

Gilt bronze.

Chandelier, probably German, towards 1800.

34 Second so-called Court Garden Room

Tapestries

Two hangings from the Rinaldo and Armida series of the Gobelin Manufactory Paris, Jacques Neilson after designs by Charles Coypel, after 1762.

Belonging to the series beginning in Room 33: Angelica's Wedding (dated 1763) and Armida destroys her Magic Castle (on the window pier).

Paintings

Franz Bernhard Frey: Pastel portrait of Max IV Joseph of Palatine-Zweibrücken, 1784.

Johann Wilhelm Hoffnas: Duke Christian IV of Palatine-Zweibrücken, 1770/1780.

Furnishings

Writing secretary (entrance wall), by Abraham Roentgen, Neuwied towards 1770.
Rosewood, kingwood, ebony rods and various coloured woods.

Writing secretary (exit wall) with inlaid Chinese scenes, by Abraham and David Roentgen, Neuwied about 1775.
Sectioned maple (stained), Amboina wood, rosewood and various coloured woods.

Commode, Jean-Baptiste Galet, signed, Paris about 1777.
Veneer of rosewood, amaranth and stained maple with marquetry urns and hunting trophies of box. Maple top, replaced. - On top:

Portal clock, Paris, around 1780.
Gilt bronze, alabaster, clockwork by Le Paute horloger du Roy, Paris. The clock probably comes from the Koblenz Palace.

Console table, Munich around 1800.
Copy of the Parisian console tables of François-Joseph Duret in Room 36. Beech, limewood, carved and gilded. Marble top replaced. Gilding probably renewed c. 1867 by the company Franz Radspieler in Munich. - On top:

Two table lamps, Paris c. 1800.
Gilt bronze.

Standing clock, Paris c. 1780.
Gilt bronze, alabaster. Clockwork by Cronier, Paris.

Four armchairs from a 14-piece suite, Paris c. 1770/75.
Beech, carved and gilded. Tapestry coverings after motifs by François Boucher and Jean-Baptiste Oudry, Jacques Neilson, Gobelins Manufactory, Paris (as in Room 33).

Two pairs of sconces, Paris, c. 1770.
Gilt bronze.

Chandelier, c. 1780.

35 Cabinet

Tapestry

From the Rinaldo and Armida series of the Gobelin Manufactory Paris, Jacques Neilson, after a design by Charles Coypel, woven by Jacques Neilson, after 1762 (see Rooms 33/34).
Armida's Fainting Spell.

Paintings

Two pastoral scenes and one domestic scene. Probably German, late 18th century (pastel).

Johann Christian Mannlich: Duke Karl II August of Palatine-Zweibrücken, 1784 (sketch).

Bust-length Portrait of an unknown gentleman, German about 1780 (pastel).

Furnishings

Table en chiffonnière (small oval table), Paris about 1760/70.
Veneer and marquetry still life on table top of rosewood, kingwood, maple and box. Gilt bronze fittings.

Bonheur du jour (small ladies writing table), attributed to Roger Vandercruse Lacroix, Paris about 1770/75.
Veneer of kingwood and rosewood with marquetry utensils of box. Gilt bronze fittings.

Vanity table (Poudreuse), probably Palatinate (studio Jakob Kieser, Mannheim) about 1770-1775.
Rosewood, kingwood.

Sofa and four armchairs, Georges Jacob, signed, Paris 1781/82.
From a suite for a cabinet in Karlsberg Castle. Walnut, beech, carved and gilded. Coverings: Tabour embroidery in coloured silk, transferred to new silk atlas, Paris 1781/82.

Vanity table, possibly Mannheim around 1770.
Stained maple. Rich marquetry work (flowers, coffee-service, playing cards and writing utensils) on coloured woods.

Three sconces, Paris, about 1770.
Gilt bronze.

Chandelier, c. 1780.
Gilt bronze, white and blue glass. Probably from the Koblenz Palace of the Elector Clemens Wenzeslaus of Treves.

36 Bedroom

Paintings
Rear wall: King Max I Joseph and his wife Karoline, Munich c. 1820 (pastels).

Entrance wall: Attributed to Johann Baptist Hoechle: Elector Max IV Joseph (from 1806 King Max I Joseph), about 1800.

Exit wall: Johann Heinrich Tischbein: Karolina, wife of Duke Christian III of Palatine-Zweibrücken, grandmother of the brothers Karl II August and Max Joseph, 1762.

In the angles of the window side: Two pastel portraits of

Auguste Wihelmine Maria of Hesse-Darmstadt, the first wife of Max IV Joseph, probably by Johann Dryander (exit side) and an unknown artist (entrance side), c. 1785.

Furnishings

State bed, Georges Jacob, Paris 1781/82.

Walnut, carved and gilded. Textiles renewed. On the headboard monogram CA (refering to Duke Karl II August of Palatine-Zweibrücken, from whose state apartment in Karlsberg Castle, the bed came). The two large armchairs and the small console table in this room also came from the furniture in the state apartment of Karlsberg Castle.

Bed canopy, Munich c. 1810.

The hangings are still made of the original cloth from Karlsberg Castle (lampas, with original trimming fringes), probably Lyons around 1780/82.

Two console tables with flower garlands, François-Joseph Duret, Paris 1781.

From a salon in Karlsberg Castle. Oak, pearwood, limewood, carved and gilded. Marble tops replaced. - On top:

(At the left): Two oval incense burners, Paris c. 1756.

Gilt bronze. Probably from the Hôtel de Deux-Ponts in Paris furnished by Pierre Patte about 1770.

(At the right): Large clock with the group "Minerva instructs Karl II August of Palatine-Zweibrücken", Paris after 1775.

Gilt bronze.

Small console table, Georges Jacob, Paris 1781/82.

From the state bedroom in Karlsberg Castle. Oak, carved and gilded. White marble top.

Two large armchairs, Georges Jacob, signed, Paris 1781/82.

From the state bedroom of Karlsberg Castle. Maple, carved and gilded. Brocade from the late 19th century transferred to renewed coverings. The monograms CA and M refer to Duke Karl II August and Duchess Maria Amalia of Palatine-Zweibrücken.

Two armchairs, George Jacob, signed, Paris 1781/82.
From a suite from the Salon des Compagnie in Karlsberg Castle. Walnut, carved and gilded. Coverings replaced.

Chandelier, c. 1780.

37 Cabinet (so-called Puille Cabinet) *Fig. 33*

In 1799-1800 Charles-Pierre Puille built two cabinets (consisting of wall panellings from Karlsberg Castle) into the suite of the "Trierzimmer" (Treves Rooms) in the East Wing of the Imperial Courtyard, at about the spot where Room 50 now stands. As a result of war damage the adjoining cabinets were cleared, and the original room decoration from about 1610/20 was revealed. Consequently, the rescued panels were not replaced where they had been before the war, but rather were added instead to the new Court Garden Rooms in the Charlotte Wing in 1966, and combined there into a single cabinet.

Carved elements from Karlsberg Castle have been incorporated into the framework of the panelling and into the door leaves. The door panel decoration (in addition to wood also modelling compound) originates from Charles-Pierre Puille from about 1799/1800. About 1867 under Ludwig II, the wooden panels with the pastel portraits were inserted replacing the earlier textile hangings. These panels had previously been located in the area of the chambers of Henriette Adelaide. All modelled parts are gilded. On the rear wall is a replacement marble mantelpiece with a mirror above.

The pastels show the Elector and the Electress of Saxony, six of their fifteen children, three princesses of Modena as well as three other princely portraits.

Entrance wall

(Middle): Marie Maximilienne de Silvestre: Friedrich August II, Elector of Saxony, as August III King of Poland (1696-1763), painted after 1745 after the original by Anton Raphael Mengs. - *(Left, from top to bottom)*: Rosalba Carriera: Anna Amalie Josepha, Princess of Modena (1699-1778), 1723. - Rosalba Carriera: Elisabeth Christine of Braunschweig-Wolfenbüttel, wife of Emperor Karl VI (1691-1750), 1730/31. - Marie Catherine de Silvestre: Franz Xaver, Prince of Saxony (1730-1806), 1740/42. - *(Right from top to bottom)*: Marie Catherine de Silvestre: Marie Christina, Princess of Saxony (1735-1782), 1740/42. - Rosalba Carriera: Henriette Maria Sophia, Princess of Modena (1702-1777), 1723. - Marie Catherine de Silvestre: Klemens Wenzeslaus, Prince of Saxony (1739-1812), 1740/42.

Exit wall

(Middle): Marie Maximilienne de Silvestre: Maria Josepha, Electress of Saxony (1699-1757), after 1743. - *(Left, from top to bottom)*: Marie Catherine de Silvestre: Maria Elisabeth, Princess of Saxony (1736-1818), 1740/42. - Johann Christian von Mannlich: Amalie, Princess of Palatine-Zweibrücken, wife of Elector Friedrich August III of Saxony (1742-1828), c. 1784. - Marie Catherine de Silvestre: Karl Christian, Prince of Saxony (1733-1797), 1740/42. - *(Right, from top to bottom)*: Rosalba Carriera: Benedicta Ernestine Maria, Princess of Modena (1697-1777), 1723. - Rosalba Carriera: Wilhelmine Amalie of Braunschweig-Lüneburg, widow of Emperor Joseph I, mother of the Saxon Electress Maria Josepha (1673-1742), 1730/31. - Marie Catherine de Silvestre: Friedrich Christian, Prince of Saxony (1722-1763), 1740/42.

Furnishings

Two armchairs and two chairs, Paris c. 1780/85.

Maple, beech, carved and gilded. Coverings with pheasant motifs: Silk lampas, brocades, after designs by Philippe de Lasalle, Pernon Manufactory, Lyon.

Fireplace screen, Georges Jacob, signed, Paris about 1780/82.

Beech, limewood, carved and gilded. Covering with pheasant motifs: Silk lampas brocaded, after designs by Philippe de Lasalle, Pernon manufactory, Lyon. (See the fireplace screen in Room 27).

Two sconces, probably Paris about 1780.
Gilt bronze.

Chandelier, about 1780.

38 Connecting Room

Surviving section of the elongated passage erected under Duke Maximilian I in the early years of the 17th century. The vault stuccowork (restored in 1958) dates from that time.

Painting

Kaspar Pitz: Duke Karl II August of Palatine-Zweibrücken (depicted as the commander of the Regiment "Royal-Deux-Ponts", which had just returned from the American Revolutionary War), signed and dated Paris 1783.
Karl II August was the elder brother of Max Joseph, and built Karlsberg Castle near Homburg, from which a large part of the furniture in the so-called "Court Garden Rooms" comes. After the death of Karl II August in 1975, Max Joseph became his legal successor and as such became Elector after the death of Karl Theodor in 1799 and King of Bavaria in 1806.

Lighting fixture

Hanging lamp, painted red and black in the style of Greek vase painting, c. 1800.
Alabaster and gilt bronze.

39-41 Charlotte Chambers

From 1814 to 1816, Charlotte Auguste, daughter of King Max I Joseph, lived in this suite of the Fountain Courtyard. She married the Duke (later King) Wilhelm I of Württemberg in 1808. In 1814, the marriage was dissolved. In 1816, she remarried the Emperor Franz I of Austria (Empress Charlotte Auguste).
In remembrance of her Munich domicile, the Charlotte Cham-

bers were restored from 1920 to 1925. Since half of the suite was occupied by the former Court Garden Rooms during the reconstruction of that suite in 1966, only Room 39-41 remained as "Charlotte Chambers"; these were fitted with furniture from the early 19th century (Wall hangings and some of the window decorations were replaced in 1966).

39 Bedroom

New green silk wall-hanging from original designs.

Paintings

Entrance wall, window side: Probably Joseph Stieler: One of the children of Eugène de Beauharnais and Auguste Amalie, probably about 1810.

Entrance wall, opposite side: Portrait of an unknown child, beginning of the 19th century.

Exit wall, window side: Joseph Stieler: Josephine Princess of Leuchtenberg, eldest child of Eugène de Beauharnais and Auguste Amalie, 1810.

Exit wall, opposite side: The later King Maximilian II as a child, German c. 1820.

Window wall: Probably Joseph Stieler: Five children (Josephine, Eugenie, August, Amalie, Theodolinde) of Eugène de Beauharnais and Auguste Amalie, c. 1815.

Furnishings

Tiled stove, cylindrical, Munich about 1800.

Bed, Munich about 1810.

Mahogany with bronze fittings. The coronet of the bed canopy is likewise of mahogany. The canopy hangings have been replaced.

Small vanity table, Munich c. 1815.

Amaranth with bronze fittings. Attachment with oval porcelain top, which shows the portraits of the five children of Eugène de Beauharnais and Auguste Amalie, copied from the painting of Joseph Stieler (see above) by the Viennese porcelain painter Leopold Lieb in 1815. - On top:

Two jugs, perhaps Italian, early 19th century.

Alabaster with bronze mounts.

Small table, about 1810-1820.

Amaranth with bronze fittings, marble top.

Table, formerly vanity table (attached mirror is missing), about 1810-1820.

Amaranth with bronze fittings, marble top.

On the tables: Two large candelabra, Paris early 19th century.

Bronze, part gilded.

Small candlestick, probably Vienna, early 19th century.

Bronze, part gilded.

Three ornamental vases, probably Paris, early 19th century.

Gilt bronze.

Two jugs (as on the small vanity table), perhaps Italian, early 19th century.

Wardrobe, probably Munich about 1810.

Mahogany with bronze decoration. Two gouaches set into the doors: Dawn and Night. - On top:

76

Crater-shaped porcelain vase, Nymphenburg Manufactory, c. 1800-1810.

Longcase clock, Vienna(?), beginning of the 19th century.
Pearwood, shaped like a fluted column, with bronze mounts. Surmounted by sculpture in white marble: Child with Dove, signed: L. Pampaloni 1833.

Two armchairs and two chairs, Paris about 1810.
Mahogany with bronze fittings. Coverings replaced.

Four sconces, Claude Galle, Paris about 1810.
Gilt bronze.

Chandelier, probably Paris c. 1810/15.

40 Music Room
New blue silk hangings after original designs.
Draperies original (satin embroidered, with original trimming fringes).

Paintings on the rear wall
Buonaventura Genelli (attributed) after Giovanni Antonio Bazzi, named Il Sodoma: Alexander the Great marries Roxane, early 19th century.
Friedrich Rehberg: Homer and the Muse, about 1810.
Friedrich Rehberg: Venus and Cupid, signed and dated Rome 1808.

Paintings on the side walls
Giambattista Bassi: Italian Landscape, signed and dated 1818.
Giambattista Bassi: View of San Vito, Rome about 1810/20.

Painting on the window pier
Friedrich Rehberg: Orpheus and Eurydice, about 1810.

Furnishings

Tiled stove, cylindrical, Munich c. 1800.

Small writing secretary, Paris c. 1800.
Amaranth with bronze fittings. - On top:

Porcelain vase, probably Nymphenburg, beginning of the 19th century.

Game table, c. 1800.
Mahogany with bronze fittings as well as ebony and ivory inlays.

Sofa and two chairs in tub form, German, about 1805.
Yew-wood with inlays, bronze fittings, coverings replaced.

Four taborets, German or French about 1805.
Yew-wood, bronze fittings, coverings replaced.

Five sconces, probably Paris about 1810.
Gilt bronze.

Large, five-piece wheel chandelier, German about 1800.

Musical instruments

Upright spinet (giraffe), Gregor Deiß, signed, Munich about 1810/20 *(Fig. 34)*.
Walnut, gilded carving, gilt bronze.

Table spinet (with drawer for sewing requisites), Joseph Klein, Vienna about 1800.
Walnut, painted medallion with maple and coloured woods.

Pedal harp, Franz Xaver Röhrer, Munich, early 19th century.
Painted red and gold.

Pedal harp, Erard Frères, signed, Paris between 1804 and 1815.
Painted yellow and gold.

Piccolo harp, probably Franz Xaver Röhrer, Munich, early 19th century.
Painted red and gold.

41 Reception Room

New yellow silk hangings after original designs.

Paintings

Rear wall: Copy after Joseph Stieler: Josephine, daughter of Eugène de Beauharnais and Auguste Amalie, as Crown Princess of Sweden, 1832.

Entrance wall: Joseph Stieler: Amalie of Oldenburg, Queen of Greece, 1836/37.

Exit wall: Adolf Henning after Joseph Stieler: Elisabeth of Bavaria, Queen of Prussia, Berlin 1846.
Eugène de Beauharnais, Duke of Leuchtenberg, German c. 1820.
Eugène de Beauharnais, stepson of Napoleon, married in 1806 the eldest daughter of King Max I Joseph, Auguste Amalia.

On the window pier: Karl von Sales: Empress Charlotte Auguste in the coronation robes, 1818.
Charlotte Auguste, daughter of Max I Joseph, fourth wife of Emperor Franz I of Austria; following her marriage to the emperor she adopted the name Karoline Auguste. The chambers bear her name.

Lithographs

Six tall oval portraits of the daughters of King Max I Joseph from chalk sketches made by Joseph Stieler probably in 1812;

from left to right: Elisabeth, Marie, Amalie, Sophie, Luise, Caroline.

Furnishings
Two commodes, probably Paris c. 1800.
Mahogany and thujawood, painted dark green. Marble tops. - On top:

Two pairs of candlesticks, possibly Vienna, about 1800-1810.
Bronze, part gilded.

Table vase, probably Paris about 1800/10.
Gilt bronze.

Mantelpiece clock, Paris about 1800.
Gilt bronze. Clockwork signed B & B à Paris.

Table, c. 1810.
Mahogany with gilt bronze fittings.

Sewing table, oval, c. 1810-1820.
Mahogany with gilt bronze appliqués.

Sofa and six armchairs, South German(?) about 1810.
Mahogany with bronze fittings. Coverings replaced.

Two sconces, probably Paris about 1800-1820.
Gilt bronze.

Chandelier, Paris c. 1810/15.

42 Charlotte Corridor
The corridor originally led to the medieval "Neuveste". Today it leads into the foyer of the Old Residence Theatre (in Klenze's former Apothecary Block), which is not accessible from here.

The (restored) stucco work dates from the building period of 1613 to 1615. It was modelled by Antonio Castelli, probably on designs by Hans Krumper.

Through the window: View into the

APOTHECARY COURTYARD

Originally the moated castle, called "Neuveste", built in 1385, was located here. Under Maximilian I, its interior courtyard was opened on the west side and connected to the large rectangular courtyard of the early 17th century.

Features surviving from this period are the western wing (containing the Treves Corridor and the Treves Rooms) and the southern wing, where the visitor is now standing. The north and east wings are structures from the time of King Ludwig I, created by Leo von Klenze from 1835 to 1842.

Small bronzes

Minerva, Munich(?) perhaps second half of the 17th century.
After a model by Alessandro Vittoria, Venice c. 1600.

Jupiter on the Eagle, Munich(?) perhaps second half of the 17th century.
After an unknown model, probably Roman c. 1630-1640.

Vestal Virgin, France about 1760.
After the antique statue in the Louvre, Paris.

Capitoline She-Wolf, Munich(?) perhaps second half of the 17th century.
After a statue in the manner of François Duquesnoy, which is a variant of the famous antique goup.

The Gaul and his Wife, Munich(?) perhaps second half of the 17th century.
After a Flemish statue c. 1640, which freely varies the antique group.

Hercules slays Cachus, Munich(?) perhaps second half of the 17th century.
After a statue from the school of Hubert Gerhard, Munich c. 1600.

Lion, pulling down a Horse, Munich(?) perhaps second half of the 17th century.
After a Netherlandish model from the early 17th century.

Reclining Beggar, Munich(?) perhaps second half of the 17th century.
After a Flemish model of 1620-1630.

Paintings

Christierna of Denmark (1521-1590), wife of Duke Franz I of Lorraine; around 1580/90.

Violante Margarethe of Savoy (1635-1663), wife of Duke Ranuccio Farnese, sister of the Electress Henriette Adelaide; c. 1660.

Christina of France (1606-1663), wife of Duke Victor Amadeus of Savoy; c. 1660.

Catherine of Spain (1567-1597), wife of Duke Carl Emanuel I of Savoy; late 16th century.

Duke Carl Emanuel I of Savoy (1562-1630); first quarter of the 17th century.

Probably Louise of Savoy (1629-1692), wife of Duke Maurice of Savoy, sister of the Electress Henriette Adelaide; c. 1660.

Duke Maurice of Savoy (1593-1657); middle of the 17th century.

43 Landing of the Broad Stairs

Tapestry

From a series "History of the Bavarian Dukes", Munich Gobelin Manufactory under Louis-Arnould d'Arondeau, between 1730 and 1770.

Balthasar Augustin Albrecht supplied the cartoons after the paintings from the early years of the 17th century by Hans Werl (now for the most part in the Burghausen Castle) formerly in the Old Hercules Hall (now the Max Joseph Hall).

Duke Johann III of Bavaria defeats the rebellious Liegers (1408), dated 1753.

Bronze sculpture

Neptune on a Dolphin, Georg Petel, cast by Wolfgang II or Christoph Neithart, Augsburg 1629-1630 (see also the painting in Room 102, which shows the earlier position in the Royal Palace Courtyard).

44 Broad Stairs

An arched structure with columns and marble balustrades separates the old flight of stairs from the time of Maximilian I. The stuccowork belongs to the construction period (1610-1615).

On the first landing a red marble panel commemorates the Golden Wedding of King Ludwig III and Queen Marie Therese of Bavaria.

45 Vestibule to the Hall of the Knights of St. George

The irregularly shaped, approximately triangular room behind the north-western gable façade of the Fountain Courtyard lost its rich stuccowork in 1944. The present stuccowork was created in 1957-1958.

Tapestries

From the series "History of the Bavarian Dukes", Munich Gobelin Manufactory under Louis-Arnould d'Arondeau, between 1730 and 1770 (see also Room 43).

Duke Heinrich of Lower Bavaria defeats King Ottokar of Bohemia (1266) dated 1758.

Wilhelm II of Lower Bavaria, Straubing and Holland defeats the Frisians (1396), dated 1762.

The Imperial Courtyard Complex of the Munich Residence

The building activity under Duke Maximilian I (reigned from 1597 to 1651, Elector from 1623) reached its artistic peak in a monumental palace complex arranged around the Imperial Courtyard in the north-western part of the Residence area. The simpler and more dignified building recapitulates the references of direction of the former Residenz, which seem in comparison to it rather manifold. The years 1612 to 1616 encompassed the construction period; upon the outbreak of the Thirty Years War, the complex was substantially complete. Artistic director of the work was the Court Art Superintendent Hans Krumper. His associates were the building engineer Heinrich Schön the Younger and the painter Peter Candid (Pieter de Witte). The unity and consistency of the work prevent us from distinguishing between the various hands; there can be no doubt that Duke Maximilian exercised an enormous influence on the conception.

The Imperial Court Complex overcame the restriction and smallness of previous living habits. A new palace type formulated by the architectural theoreticians of the late 16th century, such as Jacques-Androuet Ducerceau and Heinrich Schickhardt, was expressed here: The plain four-wing plan, whose clear shape permitted a precise separation of the individual quarters. Two banquet hall complexes (in the south, the one with the Old Hercules Hall of Duke Albrecht V, today the Max-Joseph Hall, in the north with the mighty new Imperial Hall, to which the imposing and for its time remarkable Imperial Staircase leads) are united into a square by perpendicularly adjoining structures containing smaller rooms. Long corridors accompany the suites, but rather than running along the (inner) courtyard side as was usual with such layouts, they are placed on the outer sides of the structures. They thus serve to separate the interior and exterior of court life. This is reinforced by the severity of the facade architecture, characterised by the regularly spaced windows and the sparse and solemn architectural frescoes. The rooms themselves are aligned with axially arranged passages to form the room "suites", the so-called enfilade, a modern type of appartment arrangement.

Later installations and remodellings of the 18th and 19th century have changed the interior of the banquet hall wings and the façade facing the Court Garden. The destruction of World War II left, in certain cases only the containing walls. A major part of the ceiling paintings and the movable inventory survived in storage depots. Restoration of the South Wing with the Old Hercules Hall, and the current Max-Joseph Hall (as it appeared in 1814/16) was completed in 1961 (the Max-Joseph Hall was restored once more in 1985). The extraordinarily difficult restoration in the East and West Wings with the suites of the so-called Treves Rooms and Stone Rooms was concluded in 1973. The reconstruction and restoration of the northern Banquet Hall Wing (with the Four White Horses Hall, the Imperial Hall and the Imperial Staircase, Rooms 110-112) were completed in 1985.

46-53 "Trierzimmer" (Treves Rooms)

The suite located on the main storey of the eastern Imperial Courtyard Wing (1614/15) was used for important but small-scale government events; hence its original title (Council Chambers) and the subject matter of its ceiling paintings. The rooms in the northern part were originally called the "Royal Rooms", those in the south the "Ducal" or "Princely Rooms".
Freed from later installations, the ground-plan of the enfilade is uncompromisingly symmetrical. Three portals lead from the "Triergang" or Treves Corridor into the "Trierzimmer" or Treves Rooms, one at either end and one in the middle. To either side of the central vaulted room is a suite consisting of three rooms arranged in mirror-image. The wooden coffered ceilings of these rooms resemble Italian stanze of the 16th century. The allegorical cycle of the ceiling paintings by the court painter Pieter de Witte, named Peter Candid, deal with the function of the prince as the supreme temporal authority.
Tapestries and several pieces of state furniture date from the time of its construction under Maximilian I. Other furnishings belong to the late 17th century, the reign of his son, Ferdinand Maria (1651-1679).
The name "Trierzimmer" (Treves Rooms) refers to the Prince Klemens Wenzeslaus of Saxony (1739-1812), who was brother of the Electress Maria Anna, Elector and Archbishop of Treves, Bishop of Augsburg, Freising and Regensburg as well as Provost of Ellwangen. He frequently resided for long periods in these rooms as a guest.

46 "Triergang" (Treves Corridor)

Formerly a portico with arcades opening to the east, to the Apothecary Courtyard. The open arches were closed by large windows under Prince Regent Luitpold (reigned from 1886 to 1912). The stuccowork has been restored after its partial destruction. Inserted into the interior wall there are three stucco portals made to simulate marble (the middle one original, the others heavily restored) and four two-part windows opening onto the Treves Rooms.

47 Hall of the Prince (Knights' Hall)

The room appears as it would have done around 1615. Damaged during the war, both the stucco frieze and the coffered ceiling have been faithfully restored after the original designs. The ceiling contains the monograms of the builder, Maximilian I and his first wife Elisabeth of Lorraine. Ceiling pictures by Peter Candid, probably c. 1615-1620.

Motto: "Princeps (debet esse non solum) armis decoratus, sed etiam legibus armatus (ut utrumque tempus recte possit gubernare) et bellorum et pacis", translated: The prince should be adorned not only with arms, but also armed with the laws, so that he is able to master correctly both courses of time, those of war and those of peace.

In the middle painting: The prince with Field Marshal's baton and code of laws. In the circular pictures to the sides, as allegories of war and peace: (at the head of the prince) the armed and the guardian of the laws; (at the prince's feet) host approaching a burning city (war), as well as an elegant couple in a extensive and airy garden scene (peace).

The themes of arms, law, war and peace supplement the paintings of the frieze (works of assistants). The frieze painting on the entrance wall at the left "Review of the troops", not until 1800/10, probably by Robert von Langer (1783-1843).

Tapestries

From the Month Series after cartoons by Peter Candid, woven in the Munich Tapestry Manufactory (1610-1614). They bear the Munich city hall mark as well as the signature and the weaver's mark of the manufactory-manager Hans van der Biest. The depictions of the months woven with wool, silk and gold threads show scenes from the life of the lower and upper classes with the activities characteristic for the individual months. Common to all of them are the division and framing of the picture field with climbing leaves on trunks, the coats of arms of Bavaria and Lorraine, the monograms of Maximilian I and of his first wife Elisabeth of Lorraine, as well as the cartouches with Latin sentences in hexameters pertaining to the months.

(To the left of the entrance, beginning on the southern narrow wall):

January: Banquet of a distinguished group of people, in the background, the kitchen (1613).

February: Card and dice games and bagpipe player; in the views at the left Carneval fun with sleigh ride, at the left pruning the trees (1613).

March: Field work with ploughing, sowing and harrowing; in the background pruning the grape vines (1612).

April: Refined lady and retinue hawking; in the middleground at the right falconer with hawk on carrying frame, in the background angler *(Fig. 10).*

Bronzes

On the window wall

Aeneas and Anchises, Munich(?), perhaps second half of the 17th century.

After a group from the school of Hubert Gerhard, from about 1595.

Cimon and Pera (Caritas Romana), Munich(?) perhaps second half of the 17th century.

After a Netherlandish group of 1620/30.

On the tables:

Hercules and the Hydra, Munich(?) perhaps second half of the 17th century.

Variant of the Hercules Fountain in Augsburg after a model of c. 1630.

Wrestler group after the antique, Florence, early 17th century.

Furniture

Cabinet, probably Johann Georg Esser and Wolfbauer, Augsburg c. 1680 *(Fig. 9).*

Frame with atlantes and caryatids in gilt bronze as well as carved dolphins; Tortoise-shell veneer with inlays of mother-of-pearl, copper and brass as well as semi-precious stone and marble intarsias (pietra dura), mounts of the small columns in gilt bronze (counterpart in Room 53).

Two tables, Munich c. 1610/20.

Frames in blackened pearwood with decoration in stucco made to simulate marble in flamed molding frames (the scagliola tops belonging to them were destroyed in 1944, the marble tops are replacements).

Two armchairs, North Italy, early 17th century.

Walnut, covering replaced.

48 Hall of Justice (Audience Chamber)

The room appears as it would have done around 1615. Stucco frieze restored, coffered ceiling replaced. In the window reveal painting remnant. Ceiling paintings by Peter Candid, probably 1615-1620.

Motto: "In sanctitate et iustitia", alluding to divine and temporal law. The divine law is embodied by the receiver of the heavenly law tablet, secular justice by the figure of Justitia with scales. - The frieze pictures are works of assistants (in some cases not painted and only added in the early 19th century after the room had been remodelled): Religious and secular historical codification of law (the legal system).

Tapestries

From the Month Series after cartoons by Peter Candid, Munich Tapestry Manufactory (1610-1614), with assistance by Hans van der Biest (as in Room 47).

From the right to the left:

May: Gardeners and ladies in court park. In the background pergola, at the right the Munich Court Garden and the north-east corner of the "Neuveste" (1612).

June: Sheep shearing, in the background hay harvest (1612).

July: Refined lady with retinue on a deer hunt in a river valley (1612).

Bronzes

Antinous and Minerva, both Munich(?) perhaps second half of the 17th century, after Tiziano Aspetti.

Furniture

Ornate table, Augsburg or Munich c. 1660/70.
Table top: Inlay work in Tortoise-shell and mother-of-pearl on ebony. Table frame from around 1670-1690: Ebony and three-dimensional carving in Limewood, silvered and gilded.

Four chairs with the monogram of the Elector Ferdinand Maria, Munich about 1670.
Carved walnut. Covering replaced.

49 Southern Anteroom

Originally two smaller rooms were located here (a cabinet on the courtyard side and a bedroom on the corridor side), whose original furnishings were lost in the 18th century.
The ceiling painting in the original cabinet represented an allegory of harmony (lost); the frieze paintings showed Minerva and Neptune (not preserved) as well as the closing of the Janus Temple as symbol of peace (see the painting in Room 106). About 1730, the cabinet, together with the adjacent room, was transformed into a large "bedroom", with carvings and stuccowork probably after a design by François Cuvilliés the Elder. From 1970 to 1973, the room, which had been destroyed during the war, was rebuilt and decoratied with its stucco frieze and coffered ceiling based on original designs to resemble the appearance of the other rooms from the period about 1615. Remnants of painting in the window arch.

Tapestries

Scenes from the history of the Old Testament King Saul, studio of Frans Geubel, Brussels, middle of the 16th century.
Wool and silk.
Saul's Birth (at the right).
Saul's Election as King (at the left).

Bronzes

On the window wall:

Samson slaying two Philistines, Munich(?) perhaps second half of the 17th century.
After a group by Michelangelo and Pierino da Vinci.

Tarquinius and Lucretia, Munich(?) perhaps second half of the 17th century.
After a model by Giovanni Bologna, c. 1600.

On the rear wall:

Silenus with Bacchus as a boy, Florence around 1700, perhaps after Massimiliano Soldani Benzi.

Furniture

Two armchairs with monogram of the Elector Ferdinand Maria, probably Munich about 1670.
Carved walnut. Covering replaced.

50 Entrance Hall

Vault restored from surviving remnants. Towards 1800, two cabinets were inserted here (today - combined into one cabinet - in the Charlotte Chambers, Room 37). The part of the room towards the "Triergang" (Treves Corridor) was a storage room. To the south and north of this articulated vaulted space - originally the main entrance to the Council Chambers of Maximilian I - are the flat-ceilinged rooms which are laid out in mirror image.

Paintings

Studio of Peter Candid (Hans Brüderl): Grape Harvest, Grain Harvest, Fish Catch, Cultivation of Olive Trees, 1613/15.
These belong to a series of ceiling paintings, which in the 17th century was accommodated in the rooms on the Fountain Courtyard (see Rooms 33-41).

Furniture

Six folding chairs, walnut, probably German, 16th century.

51 Northern Antechamber

As in the case of Room 49, two small rooms were originally located here. Their original decoration was lost in the 18th century. Furnished as "Chinese Cabinet" c. 1730 (wall coverings and furnishings are today in Room 63).

The ceiling painting destroyed at this time and the frieze paintings (some of which survive) showed the divinities of good fortune, public safety, general happiness and state welfare (see painting in Room 106). The room today matches the other rooms with its stucco frieze and coffered ceiling based on the original designs. Remnants of paintings in the window arch.

Tapestries

Scenes from the history of King Saul of the Old Testament, studio of Frans Geubel, Brussels, middle of the 16th century (see Room 49).

Wool and silk.

Saul receives News of the Approach of the Philistines (at the right).

Saul inspects the Building of the Temple (at the left).

Bronzes

On the window wall:

Winter, Munich(?) perhaps second half of the 17th century, after Alessandro Vittoria.

Abundantia, Munich(?) perhaps second half of the 17th century, after Alessandro Vittoria.

On the rear wall:

Venus Medici, style of Hubert Gerhard, about 1620.

52 Hall of Decision (Audience Room)

The room appears as it would have done around 1615. Restored stucco frieze, coffered ceiling replaced. Ceiling paintings by Peter Candid, probably 1615-1620.

Themes: Delectus, the Selection, and Diiudicatio, Consideration (with the aim of arriving at a good decision). The frieze paintings of the early 19th century, probably by Johann Amandus Wink and Robert von Langer, replaced an earlier cycle from 1615/20.

Tapestries

From the Month Series after cartoons by Peter Candid, Munich Tapestry Manufactory (1610-1614) under Hans van der Biest (as in Rooms 47 and 48).

From left to right:

August: Cutting grain, in the middleground catching quails or partridges with the net, in the background city view of Munich (1613).

September: Farmers bring the fruits of the harvest to the city; in the middleground hare hunt, in the background city view of Ingolstadt (1613).

October: Grape harvest and grape pressing; in the background view of Landshut, the wine cultivation area of Bavaria at that time (1612).

Bronzes

Seated Venus looking upwards, Munich(?) perhaps second half of the 17th century.

After a statue by Adriaen de Vries of 1603.

Abundantia, Munich(?), perhaps second half of the 17th century.

After the model of a Netherlandish-Italian master of 1620/30.

Furniture

Ornate table *(Fig. 12);* top has inlay work (pietra dura) in semiprecious stone and marble: Florence 1623-1627/30; frame of scagliola (on iron frame): Probably by Wilhelm Pfeiffer (Fistulator), Munich 1627/30-1635.

Four armchairs, North Italy, early 17th century.

Walnut, part gilded, with old leather coverings.

53 Council Hall

The room appears as it would have done around 1615. Stucco frieze (coats of arms of Bavaria and Lorraine in the window niches) restored, coffered ceiling renewed. In two window reveals, remnants of the original painting. Ceiling paintings by Peter Candid, probably 1615-1620.

Painting in the centre: Consilium, allegory of the good advisor. In the circular paintings: Personifications of the qualities of candour (Liberum) and loyalty (Fidele), fortitude (Constans) and reticence (Tacitum).

Frieze paintings (works of assistants): The counsellors of history: Metellus goes into exile, Socrates, Pompeius before Gentius, Papyrius, Darius and Charidemos, Croesus and Solon, Rehabeam and his advisors, Joseph's dream interpretation.

Tapestries

From the Month Series after cartoons by Peter Candid, Munich Tapestry Manufactory (1610-1614) under Hans van der Biest (as in Rooms 47, 48 and 52).

November: Boar hunt with hounds (in the middleground noble lady with retinue) and woodsmen in forest landscape (1613).

December: Hog slaughtering and sausage making, at the right flax beating; in the background view of Straubing (1613).

Bronzes

Marcus Aurelius, reduced copy of the equestrian statue on the Capitol in Rome, Rome, middle of the 16th century.

Naked myrmidon from a flagellation group, Munich(?) perhaps second half of the 17th century.

After a statue by Willem Tetrode, called Guglielmo Fiammingo, c. 1580.

94

Furniture

Cabinet, probably Johann Georg Esser and Wolfbauer, Augsburg c. 1680.

Frame with carved and gilded telamones and caryatids and as intertwined dolphins; tortoise-shell veneer with inlays of mother-of-pearl, silver, brass and copper as well as semi-precious stone and marble intarsias (pietra dura); mounts of the columns in gilt bronze (counterpart in Room 47).

Two ornate tables, Augsburg c. 1675/80.

Centre-piece of the top: Semi-precious stone and marble intarsias (pietra dura); framing in "Boulle" technique with mother-of-pearl, silvered brass, copper and Tortoise-shell (in the frame of the right-hand table signature of the silver cabinet-maker Johann Georg Esser and of the cabinet-maker Wolfbauer, Augsburg). Supporting frame with carved and gilded caryatids and dolphins, foot molding in tortoise-shell veneer.

Two armchairs and three chairs, North Italy(?) middle of the 17th century.

Walnut, covering replaced.

THE RETURN ROUTE LEADS BACK INTO THE ANTEROOM OF THE HALL OF THE KNIGHTS OF ST. GEORGE (ROOM 45). HERE CIRCULAR TOUR I CONTINUES.

54 Hall of the Knights of St. George

The rich decoration of c. 1729, the year this order of the Old Bavarian House of the Wittelsbach was reconstituted, was removed in the second half of the 19th century. After damage inflicted during World War II only the enclosing walls survived. Restoration in neutral style in 1958-1960.

Tapestries

From the series "History of the Bavarian Dukes", Munich Go-

belin Manufactory under Louis-Arnould d'Arondeau, between 1730 and 1770 (compare Rooms 43 and 45).
Duke Albrecht III of Bavaria refuses the Bohemian Royal Crown (1440), dated 1732.
Ludwig the Bavarian elected King (1314), dated 1735.

Paintings
Joseph Vivien: Four portraits of the sons of Elector Max Emanuel, brothers of the Elector Karl Albrecht: Philipp Moritz, Ferdinand Maria, Clemens August, Johann Theodor; Munich/Paris 1717-1719.

Wooden model
for a remodelling of the Munich Residence, by François Cuvilliés the Elder, 1764-1767.

Through the eastern windows view into the Fountain Courtyard.

Through the western windows view into the

CHAPEL COURTYARD
The former "Jägergäßl" (Hunter's Alley), once bordered by bourgeois buildings, crossed the former Schwabing Lane (today Residenzstraße) and thus determined the layout of the Maximilianic Residence (in the early part of the 17th century).

IN ROOM 55 THE CIRCULAR TOUR II JOINS FROM THE "GEWEIHGANG" (ANTLER CORRIDOR).

55-62   Rich Rooms

The late 16th century main storey of the East and South Wing of the Grotto Courtyard Complex was given a new appearance under the Electors Max Emanuel and Karl Albrecht in 1726-1729 by Joseph Effner. After the Residence fire of 1729, the rooms of the South Wing were magnificently rebuilt from 1730 to 1733 (festive dedication in 1737) by François Cuvilliés the Elder in the spirit of the early rococo and expanded with a gallery tract ("Green Gallery"). The rooms of the East Wing ("Effner Rooms") remained and were redecorated by François Cuvilliés. The principal masters who collaborated were the stuccoist Johann Baptist Zimmermann and the court sculptors Joachim Dietrich, Wenzeslaus Miroffsky and Adam Pichler.

The rooms were largely destroyed in 1944 but parts of the wall panelling and of the movable inventory which had been stored elsewhere survived; the stuccowork of the ceiling was recreated in 1956-1960 after the original model.

55 Antechamber

Design by Joseph Effner in 1729, reworked by François Cuvilliés the Elder, after 1730.

Stuccowork and wainscots were replaced in 1958-1960 after the original model (in reduced form). It was also at this time that the wall-hangings (ciselé velvet from Genoa) were made in imitation of those on the rear wall of the Conference Room (Room 59).

Overdoor paintings

School of Titian: Four portraits of Roman Emperors.

These portraits (in their original frames), together with eight others in the adjacent rooms form a series of Emperor Portraits, which are copies of those (now lost) which Titian painted for Federigo Gonzaga, Duke of Mantua, from 1537.

Paintings on the rear wall

Joseph Vivien: Elector Max Emanuel of Bavaria, before the city of Mons, signed and dated 1706 (pastel).

Joseph Vivien: Electress Therese Kunigunde, second wife of Max Emanuel, Munich/Paris 1717-1719.

Paintings on the side walls
Abraham Janssens: Death of Acis, Antwerp c. 1620.
Daniel Saiter: Joseph and Potiphar's Wife, probably Turin c. 1690.

Paintings on the window pier
School of Joseph Vivien: Elector Karl Albrecht and his wife Maria Amalia, about 1726.

Furnishings
Stove (at the left), Antonio Chanavese, Vienna c. 1730.
Stove (at the right), Johann Georg Härtel, after a design by Joseph Effner, Passau 1733.
Both stoves reconstructed from fragments with lacking parts added in 1959-1960.

Two console tables (window wall), Munich c. 1730, style of François Cuvilliés the Elder.
Limewood, carved and gilded. Marble top (replaced). - On top:

Two three-candle girandoles, Paris c. 1775/80.
Gilt bronze, alabaster, Monogram of the Palatine Count Max Joseph of Zweibrücken.

Longcase clock with pendulum, Paris c. 1730.
Clock with group of Apollo in sun chariot of gilt bronze, probably André-Charles Boulle. Clockwork by Etienne Lenoir. Base attributed to the Maître aux Pagodes. Tortoise-shell veneer. Gilt bronze fittings. Clock and base probably do not belong together.

Commode, attributed to Jacques-Philippe Carel, Paris c. 1735.
Veneer in kingwood. Gilt bronze appliqués. Old marble top. - On top:

Porcelain vase, Japan, so-called Old-Imari, end of the 17th/beginning of the 18th century, with good luck symbols (birds of paradise, dragons, etc.)

Two taborets and four banquettes, Munich c. 1730/40.
Carved, painted white and gilded. Coverings replaced.

Mantelpiece clock with the figure of a Cupid who wakes the Bacchante (on the mantelpiece), Paris c. 1780.
Gilt bronze, alabaster. Clockwork by Jean-Louis (?) Amant, Paris.

Three chandeliers (one with Electoral Bavarian coat of arms), probably after a design by Guillielmus de Groff, Munich or Paris c. 1730.
Gilt bronze.

56 Outer Audience Room

Design by Joseph Effner in 1728, revised by François Cuvilliés the Elder after 1730.

Stucco and wainscots restored after the original model (but in reduced form) in 1958-1960. Wall hanging (Genoese ciselé velvet) rewoven after the original model in Room 59. The carved sections of the wall panelling were destroyed in 1944.

Overdoor paintings
School of Titian. Four portraits of Emperors.
The paintings, in their original frames, belong to the series beginning in Room 55.

Paintings
Paul de Vos: Two Animal Pieces, Antwerp, middle of the 17th century.

Jan Fyt: Fruit and Hunting still life with dogs and parrot, Antwerp, middle of the 17th century.

Furnishings

Bureau plat (desk), Charles Cressent, Paris c. 1730/35.
Veneer of rosewood, amaranth and satin rosewood. Gilt bronze fittings. - On top:

Two candlesticks, probably Paris c. 1770.
Gilt bronze.

Chair (at the desk), Munich c. 1750.
Limewood, carved and gilded. Covering replaced.

Commode (on the entrance wall), Charles Cressent, Paris c. 1730/35.
Veneer of rosewood, satin rosewood and amaranth. Gilt bronze fittings. Marble top replaced - On top:

Porcelain vase, Japan, so-called Old Imari, end of the 17th/beginning of the 18th century.

Large console table (rear wall), Munich c. 1725-1730, style of Joseph Effner.
Limewood, carved and gilded. Marble top replaced. - On top:

Ornate clock with St. George, Munich, probably about 1755/60.
Clockwork signed "Paulus Graff in Munich". Case with gilt bronze statuettes and ornaments as well as silver fittings. - At the sides:

Two porcelain vases (in the form of stem vases), Japan, so-called Old Imari, end of the 17th/beginning of the 18th century.

Two encoignures (corner cabinets), signed Pierre II Migeon, Paris c. 1750/55.
Veneer of rosewood and amaranth with marquetry of kingwood. Gilt bronze fittings. Marble top replaced. - On top:

Two three-branched girandoles, Paris about 1775.
Gilt bronze, alabaster (style of Etienne-Maurice Falconet).

Two console tables (in front of the window piers), design by François Cuvilliés the Elder, executed by Joachim Dietrich, Munich c. 1730.
Limewood, carved and gilded. Marble tops replaced. - On top:

Two lidded vases, Japan, so-called Old Imari, late 17th/early 18th century.

Four banquettes, two taborets, Munich c. 1730.
Limewood, carved and gilded. Coverings replaced.

Two pairs of sconces (on the window wall), probably second half of the 19th century; (on the rear wall), Paris c. 1730, in the style of Charles Cressent.
Gilt bronze.

Chandelier with Jupiter hurling Lightning Bolts, probably Munich c. 1730.
Gilt bronze.

57 Inner Audience Room

Remodelled after the fire of 1729 under supervision of François Cuvilliés the Elder.
Of the four leaf-doors, the one on the exit wall at the right is of baked and glazed clay (with stucco additions): I.e. wall of a stove heated from the outside. All of the panelling on the win-

dow wall and most of the rest is original. Carvings by Joachim Dietrich. Mirror glass replaced. Also preserved are: The old marble fireplace with wrought iron fireplace grate (19th century) and the stuccowork in the upper window reveals. Replaced (after original models): The ceiling stuccowork and the wall hangings (Genoese ciselé velvet; compare Room 59).

Wall carving

The baseboard is decorated with lattice work and tendrils, in the door panels palmettes. Fireplace panel with bonded shell-work ornaments and palmettes with masks, above Juno in the peacock chariot. On the window wall, the decorated panels are surmounted by personifications of the four seasons (Joachim Dietrich, 1734).

Ceiling stuccowork

Between lattice and shell work, putti and fabulous beasts with allegorical figures and emblems. Middle rosette (reconstructed after the original by Johann Baptist Zimmermann).

Overdoors

School of Titian: Four portraits of Emperors.
The paintings, in their original frames, belong to the series beginning in Room 55.

Overdoor (above the entrance door)

Peter Candid (Pieter de Witte): Emperor Ludwig the Bavarian, c. 1600/05.
Originally full-lengh, the portrait was moved here in 1729 whereupon it was cut down to a three-quarter-length portrait and was widened at the sides for its new context. Originally part of a cycle on the ground floor of a part of the Residence on the Residenzstrasse, c. 1600 (see Rooms 91-93).

Paintings on the walls on both sides of the entrance

Joseph Vivien: Hereditary Prince Karl Albrecht (later Emperor Karl VII) and his wife Maria Amalia, 1722.

Furnishings

Throne canopy, Munich c. 1730.
Red velvet with appliquéd gold braiding.

Throne chair, Munich c. 1750.
Limewood, carved and gilded. Original covering: Red warp velvet with appliquéd woven gold braiding.

Floor carpet, Persian knotted rug, probably 19th century.

Two commodes (entrance wall), Charles Cressent, Paris c. 1730/35 *(Fig. 22/23)*.
Veneer of amaranth and satin rosewood, gilt bronze appliqués. Marble tops replaced. - On top:

Two large lidded vessels, Japanese, Old Imari, end of the 17th/beginning of the 18th century.

Two encoignures (corner cabinets), Munich around 1740/45.
Veneer of rosewood and amaranth. Gilt bronze appliqués. Marble tops replaced. - On top:

Two girandoles with a putto (Satyr and Bacchus), Claude-Michel Clodion and Louis-Félix de Larue, Paris c. 1780.
Bronze, part gilded, alabaster.

Two console tables (window piers), after a design by François Cuvilliés the Elder, Munich c. 1730.
Limewood, carved and gilded, marble tops replaced. - On top:

Two candelabra each with two putti, Paris c. 1775, in the style of Jean-Louis Prieur.
Gilt bronze, alabaster.

Eight taborets, Munich c. 1730/40.
Coverings replaced.

On the marble mantelpiece:
Mantelpiece clock, Paris c. 1870 (in the style of a French man-
telpiece clock from the time of Louis XIV).
Gilt bronze, Tortoise-shell.

Two girandoles, Claude-Michel Clodion and Louis-Félix de
Larue, Paris c. 1780.
Counterparts to those on the encoignures.

Two sconces (at the sides of the mantelpiece mirror), Paris c.
1720/25.
Gilt bronze.

Chandelier, Paris c. 1715.
Gilt bronze.

58 The Green Gallery   *Fig. 21*

From 1731 to 1733, François Cuvilliés the Elder erected a side
wing to the complex of the Rich Rooms, its façade erected in
front of the (preserved) vestibule and the state staircase, which
led to the Green Gallery, a picture gallery, on the upper floor.
In 1764 the staircase was converted into a banquet hall on the
upper floor but was demolished in 1896. The Green Gallery
remained. When the "Königsbau" (Royal Palace) was erected
in 1826, the southern annex room was demolished and the
Green Gallery lost its originally H-shaped ground-plan. The
northern annex room lies in the suite of the Rich Rooms
adjoining the "Inner Audience Room". The stuccowork contains allusions to the imperial dignity, for which the builder,
Elector Karl Albrecht, strove successfully. The seven-bay
gallery room itself originally possessed three ceiling frescos by
Balthasar Augustin Albrecht, 1733/34, which together formed
an apotheosis of the arts and sciences under the patronage of

104

the Wittelsbach family. One of the paintings was probably damaged during the rebuilding of the Green Gallery in 1826 and was lost during the course of the 19th century. The other two were destroyed in World War II. The present central painting by Giovanni Antonio Pellegrini shows Elector Johann Wilhelm of the Palatinate as Jupiter, surrounded by allegorical figures (painted in 1713/14 for Bensberg Palace near Düsseldorf).

Johann Baptist Zimmermann was the stuccoist, Joachim Dietrich and Wenzeslaus Miroffsky were the carvers. The stuccowork was almost completely destroyed during World War II and was reconstructed from the original model. Parts of the wainscot, mirror frames and picture frames inserted into the wall (in the annex room) are original. The remaining carving is restored from the original model. Wall hanging (green silk damask) renovated after the original.

The paintings (most of them with original frames) and moveable furnishings remained completely intact.

Furnishings

Five console tables, Wenzeslaus Miroffsky after a design by François Cuvilliés the Elder, Munich c. 1733/34.
Limewood, carved and gilded. Marble top replaced. - On top:

Five East Asian lidded vases, 17th/18th century.

Two console tables (northern annexe room), modelled after the five console tables in the main room, Munich probably after 1769.
Limewood, carved and gilded. Marble top replaced. - On top:

Two dishes, China, 17th/18th century.

Ten taborets, Munich c. 1730.

Three chandeliers, Vienna c. 1870.

On the southern mantelpiece: Mantelpiece clock, Andreas Lehner, Munich c. 1730/40.
Tortoise-shell, gilt bronze. On the pendulum, coat of arms of Johann Theodor of Bavaria, Bishop of Freising and Regensburg.

On the northern mantelpiece: Mantelpiece clock, Charles Cressent, Paris c. 1730/33, clockwork by Jean-Baptiste Baillon.
Tortoise-shell, gilt bronze.

Paintings
Following the spatial division, the paintings of the transverse wing are named first and then those of the longitudinal main room. The series begins at the entrance wall and continues in clockwise direction towards the left. The paintings are listed from bottom to top.

Entrance wall
first row
Christian W. E. Dietrich (1712-1774): Sacrifice of Isaac. - Victor H. Janssens (1658-1736): Holy Family with the Infant St. John the Baptist (signed). - Flemish, 17th century: Entrance into a City. - Dutch, c. 1700: Flower piece.

Overdoor
Frans Snyders (1579-1657): Kitchen Piece.

second row
School of Jacopo Tintoretto (1518-1594): Christ and Mary Magdalene. - Luigi Garzi (1638-1721): Hagar in the Desert.

Fireplace wall
1st row
Guido Canlassi, named Cagnacci (1601-1681): St. Sebastian. - Antonio Cifrondi (1657-1730)?: Virgin and Child with St. John

106

the Baptist - Style of Luca Giordano (1632-1705): Portrait of a Man.

2nd row
Antonio Zanchi (1631-1722): Joseph presents his Brothers to the Pharaoh.

3rd row
Nikolaus Prugger (c. 1620-1694): Portrait of Balthasar Camerlocher, 1642. - Flemish, early 17th century: Portrait of a Man. - Ciro Ferri (1634-1689): Fortitude and Peace.

4th row
Nikolaus Prugger: Portrait of the Wife of Balthasar Camerlocher, 1642. - Andrea Celesti (1637-1706): Holy Family. - Erasmus Quellinus the Younger (1607-1678): Daedalus and Icarus.

5th row
Antonio Zanchi: The Good Samaritan.

6th row
Aert de Gelder (1645-1727): Oriental Man. - Venetian, 16th century: Virgin and Child with St. John the Baptist. - German, 18th century: Portrait of a Clergyman.

Wall opposite the entrance
1st row
Adam Frans van der Meulen (1632-1690): View of Dinant. - Roelant Savery (1576-1639): Paradise.

Overdoor
Frans Snyders: Still Life.

2nd row
Style of Peter Paul Rubens (1577-1640): Blessing Christ (after

North Italian painting of the 16th century). - Victor H. Janssens: Tobias and the Angel (signed). - School of Anthony van Dyck (1599-1641): Portrait of a Man. - Dutch, c. 1700: Flower Piece.

Arched wall at the left
Copy after Peter Paul Rubens: Hercules and Deianeira. - Hans von Aachen (1552-1615): Bathsheba. - Johann Georg Edlinger (1741-1819): Portrait of Countess Maria Theresia de la Rosée, 1783. - Johann Georg Edlinger: Portrait of a Girl.

Arched wall at the right
Polidoro da Lanciano (1515-1565): Virgin and Child with St. John the Baptist. - Peter Candid (c. 1548-1628): Holy Family with Infant St. John the Baptist (acquired in 1972). - German, 17th century: Portrait of a young Man with Candle. - Caspar Amort (1602-1675): Study of a Male Head.

Main room

Longitudinal wall
1st row
Jusepe de Ribera (c. 1590-1652): St. James the Greater (signed and dated 1634). - Venetian, 16th century: David with the Head of Goliath. - Copy after Domenico Zampieri, named Il Domenichino (1581-1641): Sibyl.

2nd row
Caspar de Crayer (1584-1669): Adoration of the Shepherds. - Carlo Dolci (1616-1686): St. Catherine. - Venetian or German, early 17th century: Flora.

3rd row
Simone Cantarini (1612-1648): Doubting Thomas. - Carlo Maratta (1625-1713): The Virgin Annunciate. - German or Italian, 17th century: Bearded Saint.

4th row

Copy after Paolo Veronese (1528-1588): Justice and Peace. - Carlo Maratta: The Archangel Gabriel of the Annunciation. - Style of Titian (died 1576): Portrait of a Cardinal.

5th row

Copy after Peter Paul Rubens: Holy Family with Infant St. John the Baptist and Elizabeth. - Johann J. Langenhöffel (1750-1807): Cupid and Psyche (signed and dated 1788). - North Italian (Antiveduto Grammatica?), 17th century: Virgin and Child.

6th row

Hermann Elbel (active in the second half of the 18th century): Portrait of Maria Anna Josepha Charlotte of Palatine-Sulzbach, Duchess of Bavaria, as St. Cecilia (monogr.), c. 1750. - Ferdinand Kobell (1740-1799): River Landscape (signed and dated 1792). - Italian, 17th century, style of Domenichino: St. Cecilia.

End wall with fireplace

1st row

Style of Titian: Venus. - Jan Hackaert (1629-1700): Hunting Party at a Pond in the Forest. - Jan Fyt (1611-1661): Hunting Still Life.

2nd row

Copy after Paolo Veronese: Mars and Venus. - Juriaen van Streeck (1632-1687): Still Life (signed). - Italian, 17th century: Christ as Salvator Mundi.

Window wall

1st row

Antonio Tempesta (1555-1630): Homecoming. - Paolo Farinato (1524-1606): Virgin and Child with St. John the Baptist. -

Joseph Vivien (1657-1735): Portrait of Maria Anna Carolina, Princess of Bavaria, 1717/19.

2nd row

Probably Johann Heinrich Tischbein the Elder, c. 1750: Maria Franziska Dorothea of Palatine-Sulzbach, Duchess of Zweibrücken-Birkenfeld. - Flemish, 17th century: Crucifixion. - Italian (Francesco Granacci?), 16th century: Virgin and Child with St. John the Baptist.

3rd row

Louis Silvestre the Younger (1675-1760): Maximilian Emanuel Franz Joseph of Bavaria, named Chevalier de Bavière, illegitimate son of the Elector Max Emanuel (signed and dated 1707). - Italian, 17th century: Cupid.

4th row

Jean-Marc Nattier (1685-1766): Peter the Great (signed and dated 1717). - Italian, 17th century: Charity.

5th row

Copy after Peter Paul Rubens: St. Mary Magdalene. - Nicolaes Berchem (1620-1683): Italian Seaport. - Francesco Albani (1578-1660): St. Paul.

6th row

Style of Paris Bordone (1500-1571): Venus. - Italian, 17th century: Holy Family with St. Catherine. - Jan van Neck (1636-1714): Portrait of a Lady (signed and dated 1667).

Go back through Room 57 into Room 59.

59 Conference Room

Design: François Cuvilliés the Elder, 1730; built 1731/33.
The formerly luxuriantly-carved elements were destroyed in

1944, but were reconstructed by 1983. The stucco in the upper window reveals is original, while that on the ceiling is a reconstruction from the original model. The hanging on the rear wall is original: Genoese ciselé velvet from the period c. 1730-1735. New hangings from 1958-1960 on the remaining wall surfaces. Two of the doors are tiled: i.e. walls of the stoves formerly heated from outside.

Wall carving
Continuous baseboard with strap ornament and lattice work (replaced).

Ceiling stuccowork
Early rococo forms, enlivened with figural elements of allegorical and mythological subjects (replaced).

Fireplace after a model by Johann Baptist Zimmermann, 1733.

Overdoors
Giovanni Antonio Pellegrini: The Four Fathers of the Early Church, Venice about 1730-1740.
Formerly, personifications of the four continents by Giuseppe Valeriani or Gasparo Diziani were inserted here. Overdoor frame replaced.

Furnishings
Bureau plat (desk), Bernard II Vanrisamburgh, Paris c. 1730/33.
Kingwood veneer. Gilt bronze fittings. Black leather writing surface replaced.
- On top:

Inkwell with Electoral Bavarian coat of arms, Paris c. 1730, in the style of François-Antoine Vassé.
Gilt bronze.

Chair (at the desk), Munich c. 1750-1760.
Limewood, carved and gilded. Covering replaced.

Large console table (on the rear wall), design by François Cuvilliés the Elder, c. 1730, execution by Wenzeslaus Miroffsky, Munich 1732.
Limewood, carved and gilded. Marble top replaced. - On top:

Three-piece candelabra set, Paris c. 1780.
Gilt bronze, alabaster (style of Etienne-Maurice Falconet). The ensemble comes from the Zweibrücken Palace in Strassburg.

Two encoignures (corner cabinets), Charles Cressent, Paris c. 1730/35.
Veneer of amaranth, satin rosewood and rosewood. Gilt bronze fittings. Marble top replaced. - On top:

Two porcelain cachepots (flowerpots), Japan, Old Imari, end of the 17th/beginning of the 18th century.

Two console tables (on the window wall), Munich, design by François Cuvilliés the Elder, probably executed by Joachim Dietrich, Munich c. 1730.
Limewood, carved and gilded. Marble tops replaced. - On top:

Two lidded vessels, Japan, Old Imari, 17th/18th century.

Sofa and four taborets, Munich c. 1730/35.
Limewood, carved and gilded. Original coverings on the taborets: Polychrome chenille embroidery on silver lamé, with golden braiding and gold embroidery, on red silk velvet. Covering of the sofa replaced.

On the marble mantelpiece:
Mantelpiece clock with the theme: History sacrifices Cupid, Paris c. 1780.
Clockwork by Imbert l'aîné (Jean-Gabriel Imbert). Gilt bronze, alabaster.

Two candelabra, Paris c. 1780.
Gilt bronze, alabaster (style of Etienne-Maurice Falconet).

112

Ten sconces, probably second half of the 19th century.
Gilt bronze.

Chandelier, c. 1740-1750.
Iron and bronze frame, part gilded. Cut glass pendants.

60 State bedroom *Fig. 20*

Design: François Cuvilliés the Elder, 1730.
The gilded carvings of the panelling, the doors and the
balustrade were completed by Wenzeslaus Miroffsky in 1732.
Stucco in the upper window reveals is original. The gilded stuccowork of the ceiling, replaced in 1957-1958, was created by
Johann Baptist Zimmermann (1731). - The walls are panelled
in the front part; the bed space enclosed by a balustrade (with
rounded corners) is covered in red velvet with luxurious gold
embroidery. Large wall mirrors are situated on the two window
piers and between the leaf doors; there is a marble fireplace on
the west wall.

Wall carvings
Ornaments of early rococo in bound but luxurious shapes. The
ornamental panels with strap and trellis work, acanthus and garlands are interspersed with emblems, but also birds, masks and
putti. Personificatons of the four seasons surmount the lateral
wall sections (wall section in the south-eastern corner added in
1958).

Ceiling stuccowork (copy)
On the window side: "Morning" (Apollo on the Sun Chariot
preceded by Dawn and Dew). Above the side walls: "Noon"
(Mars and Venus) and "Evening" (Diana Appears to
Endymion). Over the bed "Night" (Morpheus Descends on
Nox). On the trellis work of the cavetto, the figures of Poetry,

Painting, Geography, Astronomy, Music and the Art of War. Above the balustrade, cartouche with the monograms CA and MA (Karl Albrecht and Maria Amalia).

Wall hanging in the bed recess
Appliquéd high-relief embroidery in appliqué and scatter technique on red silk velvet, by Jean-François Bassecour, 1735.

Overdoors
Gaspare Diziani: Allegories of the Four Times of Day (Day and Evening, Night and Morning)

Furnishings
Varnished commode (entrance wall), Antoine-Robert Gaudreaus, Paris c. 1730/33.
Cladding with French and Chinese lacquer panels. Gilt bronze fittings. Marble tops from Portor (Pyrenees) from the 19th century. - On top:

Mantelpiece clock, Paris c. 1750.
Gilt bronze with soft porcelain flowers of the Mennecy-Villeroy Manufactory. Hands adorned with brilliants and rubies. Clockwork by Claude-Simon Passemant, Paris. The clock with Arabic characters and numbers was originally intended for export to Turkey.

Two varnished commodes (window wall), Bernard II Vanrisamburgh, Paris c. 1730/33.
Cladding with French varnished panels. Gilt bronze fittings. Marble tops from Portor (Pyrenees) from the 19th century. On it:

Two candelabra vases, Paris c. 1780.
Bronze, part gilded, alabaster (vase body).

Varnished writing desk, Bernard II Vanrisamburgh, Paris c. 1737.
French polish in the art of Japanese varnish. Gilt bronze fittings. - On top:

Mantlepiece clock and two candleholders with Asian figures, Paris c. 1737.

Bronze, partly gilded with coloured varnish painting. Clockwork by Julien Le Roy, Paris.

Two console tables, design by François Cuvilliés the Elder, Munich c. 1730.

Limewood, carved and gilded. Marble tops replaced. - On top:

Two Cloisonné vases, China, 18th century.

Two banquettes and four taborets, Munich c. 1730-1740.

Limewood, carved and gilded. Coverings of the two front taborets similar to that of the taborets in Room 59.

Bed and canopy new, as replacements for the richly embroidered original, fire-destroyed in 1944.

On the carved balustrade:

Six candelabra pyramids, probably Munich c. 1730.

On the mantelpiece:

Mantelpiece clock and two candelabra, Chinese porcelain of the K'ang-hsi Era (1662-1722) in gilt bronze mounts, Paris c. 1730 *(Fig. 18)*.

"Email sur biscuit". Clockwork by Charles Voisin, Paris.

Chandelier, probably Vienna, 18th century.

61 Mirror Cabinet   *Fig. 19*

Design: François Cuvilliés the Elder, 1731; carvings by Wenzeslaus Miroffsky, 1731-1732.

Of the original wall panelling, that of the rounded corners, the arch above the alcove niche and the spandrel above the window pier is preserved. The rest of the wall panelling was destroyed in 1944 and has been replaced with copies. As for the stuccowork, only that of the window niches survived; the stuccowork on the ceiling is a copy of the original by Johann Baptist Zimmermann.

Wall carving
Acanthus decorations with trellis work, garlands and palmettes, in between putti and masks.

Ceiling stuccowork (copy)
Strap and scroll work of the early rococo with putti and masks; also monogram CA and MA (Karl Albrecht and Maria Amalia) flanked by pairs of lions.

Furnishings
Lacquer Commode, Bernard II Vanrisamburgh, Paris c. 1730/33.
Cladded with French lacquered panels. Gilt bronze fittings. Marble tops from Portor (Pyrenees) from the 19th century. - On top:

Mantelpiece clock with elephant, Paris c. 1750.
Bronze, part gilded. Clockwork by Jean-Baptiste Baillon.

Writing secretary in the form of a mirror console, design by Guillielmus de Groff, Munich 1735/36; executed by Johann Michael Höcker(?).
Snakewood. The gilt bronze cartouche in the middle is a replacement.

Settee, two taborets and fireplace screen, Munich c. 1730.
Limewood, carved and gilded. Coverings: Red velvet with silk flower embroideries in gold embroidered border.

Four guéridons (candlestick stands): Augsburg c. 1729/30 and 1732/33.
Gilded silverwork by Johann Engelbrecht, Augsburg, with Meissen porcelain inlays. Decoration: Augsburg by Anna Elisabeth Wald.

Chandelier, Munich 1767.
Ivory. Made by Elector Max III Joseph of Bavaria as recorded in an inscription.

Chandelier in the mirror niche, Paris c. 1725/30.
Chinese, Japanese and early Meissen porcelain, gilt bronze mounts.

On the mantelpiece
Two candelabra, porcelain parrots, Meissen, with gilt bronze mounts, Paris c. 1740.

Porcelain vase, China c. 1700.

On the consoles of the wall panelling
Chinese and Japanese porcelain, 17th/18th century.

From the Mirror Cabinet, Room 61, a view into the Miniature Cabinet, Room 62.

62 Miniature Cabinet

Design: François Cuvilliés the Elder, 1731. Carvings by Joachim Dietrich, 1732. The walls are decorated with 128 miniature paintings by Netherlandish, French and German artists of the 16th to the 18th centuries.

All the miniatures with their finely carved frames, the two door-leaves with their extremely rich carving and the two window shutters are original.

Wall carvings

The lavishly carved walls were gutted in 1944; copies of the original carving are currnetly being prepared. The wainscots (with allegories of the four seasons) were reconstructed during the restoration campaign of 1958. On the original door leaves and window shutters: Masks and acanthus decoration with strap-work and trellis-work.

Ceiling

The decoration of the painted and stuccoed ceiling is a copy of the original from 1731-1732 (by Johann Baptist Zimmermann) made in 1958.

Furnishings

Four taborets, Munich c. 1735.
Limewood, carved, varnished in red and gilded. Tapestry coverings from the Beauvais Manufactory.

Fireplace screen, Munich c. 1735.
Limewood, carved, varnished in red and gilded. Screen panel: Coloured flowers in chenille embroidery, bordered by gold embroidery.

On the mantelpiece:

Mantelpiece clock, Paris c. 1740.
Japanese porcelain, 17th/18th century, in gilt bronze mount, parts with coloured lacquer painting (Statuette of a blackamoor).

Two guéridons, probably 18th century.
Limewood, carved and gilded; with bronze parts. - On top:

Two candelabra pyramids, c. 1720.
Porcelain parts, Japan; gilt bronze mount and pendants probably Paris.

Chandelier, South Germany (Augsburg?), end of the 17th century.

Ivory. Middle section with fully sculptured episodes from the Hercules myth. On the branches further mythological themes. Mounts: Gilded silver, Augsburg, with silversmith's mark of Johann Andreas Thelott.

Paintings

Above the mantelpiece mirror: After Charles Lebrun (1619-1690): Alexander and the Family of Darius.

The delicate original miniatures were replaced by copies for reasons of conservation.On both sides of the mirror: Maximilian de Geer (1680-1768), views of Bavarian palaces, c. 1730. On the other walls, miniature paintings by Johann Wilhelm Baur (died in 1640), Hans Bol (1534-1593), François Bouly (active in the early part of the 18th century), Paulus Bril (1554-1626), Ferdinand Carl Bruni (died in 1726), Matthias Kager (1566-1634), Johann König (1586-1642), Michael Scharner (died in c. 1677), Joseph Werner (1637-1710) and others.

The tour returns to the State Bedroom, Room 60 and from there continues in the Chinese Cabinet, Room 63.

63 Chinese Cabinet

Also called "Martyr Room". According to tradition, the corpses of the princes were dissected here; their hearts were then taken to the Pilgrimage Chapel in Altötting (since the death of Elector Maximilian I who died in 1651).

The Chinese Cabinet, installed here since 1966, belongs to the era of the Elector Karl Albrecht, but until 1944, was located in the so-called Treves Tract (see Room 51).

Wall hangings

Eleven embroidered wall hangings, probably Munich c. 1730.

Black silk taffeta with appliqués of gold and silver lamé fabrics, silk fabrics and braidings, with "needle painting" overembroidered in coloured silks.
Depictions from the life of the Chinese, adapted from engravings in illustrated travel reports of the time (probably from the work "Asia" by Olfert Dapper, which appeared in 1673).

Furnishings
Desk, eight chairs, a sofa and two taborets, Mannheim, c. 1770.
Limewood, carved; coloured varnish painting on red ground. Coverings replaced. The initials EA (for Electress Elisabeth Auguste, wife of Elector Karl Theodor) on the folding desk. From Schwetzingen Palace near Heidelberg.

Two sconces and a wall clock, Paris c. 1730-1740.
Gilt bronze with trimmings of Chinese and European porcelain. Clockwork by Voisin.

Four sconces, German(?), middle of the 18th century.
Bronze, coloured, provided with Chinese and European porcelain elements.

Chandelier, Augsburg c. 1710.
Silver chasing.

64 Cloakroom

This room was also once called the "Martyr Room", (see Room 63). Elector Max III Joseph used the room as a carpentry workshop. In accordance with its ancillary function the room was newly furnished after the Second World War with pieces of various origins.

Tapestry
"The Continence of Scipio", Munich Gobelin Manufactory under Joseph Chédeville, 1799, after a cartoon by Thomas Christian Wink (1781) .

Paintings
George Desmarées (studio): The four eldest Children of Elec-

120

tor Karl Albrecht: Maria Antonia Walburgis, Theresia Benedikta, Maximilian (III) Joseph (later Elector) and Joseph Leopold; to judge from the age of the children about 1732/33, but probably not painted until 1740.

Furnishings
Two commodes, attributed to François Lieutaud, Paris c. 1720/25.
Palisander veneer, gilt bronze fittings. - On top:

Two cachepots (flower pots), Japan, Old Imari, late 17th/early 18th century.

Six armchairs, probably German, middle of the 18th century.
Unpainted, carved oak. Coverings: Embroidery in gros and petit point (on canvas) in coloured wools and silks, c. 1730.

Chandelier, probably German, second half of the 18th century.

65 Connecting Room

This room was only created after 1944, when, as a result of war damage, the ground floor plan around the Papal Chambers (Rooms 67 - 71) was changed. Before the Second World War the Joseph Chapel was located here.

Furniture
Façade cabinet, Munich c. 1640.
Hungarian ash, maple, walnut, oak.

Paintings
Attributed to Nikolaus Prugger: Portrait of the Electress Maria Anna, c. 1657.

Probably Anna, daughter of Philipp III of Spain, wife of Louis XIII of France (1601-1666), French c. 1660.

Maria Theresia, daughter of Philipp IV of Spain, wife of Louis XIV of France (1638-1683), French c. 1660.

66 Former Fourth Summer Room

This small square room (not accessible to the public) was attached to the balcony of the first floor of the Grotto Court-yard, during the time of the Electress Henriette Adelaide. When in 1680-1685 this altana was enclosed to form a suite of rooms, the "Sommerzimmer" (Summer Rooms) on the orders of Elector Max Emanuel and in accordance with plans by the architect Henrico Zuccalli, this room was used as a "Waiting room to the beautiful Chapel" (Joseph Chapel - see Room 65 - in the apartment of Electress Henriette Adelaide), and as the fourth room of the "Sommerzimmer" Suite. It was raised in height by one storey, to bring in light from the east. When, from 1729, the Rich Rooms were built in place of the Summer Rooms, the only remaining portion of the older suite was this annexe room.

The stuccowork of the ceiling and on the walls by Prospero Breni, 1681, was preserved; the painting, probably by Antonio Triva about 1680/85 is lost.

67-71 Papal Chambers

In 1640/41, several rooms in this complex were furnished for Electress Maria Anna, the second wife of Maximilian I, and again in 1666/67 for Electress Henriette Adelaide, the wife of Ferdinand Maria (Joseph Chapel, Bedroom with alcoves, Heart Cabinet and Drawing Room, known as the Grotto Room). The private apartment of Electress Henriette Adelaide originally extended along the Residenzstrasse with state rooms (comprising two antechambers today Rooms 100-102; an audience room, today Room 71), and a gallery with two adjoining cabinets (torn down in 1827, replaced by the "Königsbau" (Royal Palace). The traditional name "Papal Chambers" refers to the visit of Pope Pius VI, who resided here in 1782. The very magnificent furnishings in North Italian baroque style with Turinese overtones were largely destroyed in 1944. The present ground-plan no longer corresponds to the pre-war arrangement.

67 Red Chamber

The ceiling paintings (originally in the so-called Grotto Room destroyed in 1944) date from 1669/73, the overdoors and the gilded carvings in the corner panels of the ceiling and the doors originate from the baroque decorations.

Ceiling paintings

Middle painting: "Triumph of Majesty and Love". - Side paintings: "Courageous Virtue" (A palm burdened with a stone during a storm), "Christian Wisdom" (Ship in storm, guided by the North Star), "Friendship" (Column entwined with wintergreen), "Steadfastness" (Reborn Phoenix arising from the ashes). -

The previous attribution of these paintings to Antonio Triva cannot be maintained; however they cannot currently be attributed to any of the court painters active in Munich at that time.

Overdoors:

Antonio Triva: Two Pairs of Putti.
Probably portraits of the children of the Elector Ferdinand Maria.

Studio of Stefano Bombelli: Elector Ferdinand Maria of Bavaria and his wife Henriette Adelaide of Savoy, c. 1670.

Elisabeth, daughter of Heinrich IV of France, wife of Philipp IV of Spain (1602-1644), c. 1620.

Henriette Maria, daughter of Henri IV of France, wife of Charles I of England (1600-1669), after Peter Lely in the style of Anthony van Dyck, c. 1632.

Furnishings
Two commodes, possibly Munich about 1730.
Veneer of amaranth, gilt bronze fittings. Marble tops replaced. - On top:

(Left): Platter, Japan, Old Imari, 17th/18th century.

(Right): Ornate shrine of the Electress Anna Maria Luisa de' Medici, studio of Giovanni Battista Foggini, Florence c. 1710.
Ebony, semi-precious stones, gilt bronze. In it: Bronze statuette of Minerva, probably Florence, early 18th century.

Two chairs, Munich about 1720.
Gilded carved frames. Covering: Relief embroidery with gold threads and gold braiding applied to green velvet: In the middle section of the backs "bizarre" silks.

68 Heart Cabinet   *Fig. 16*

As a result of the remodelling of 1667, the room acquired the character of a baroque love cabinet through the carved and painted motifs of the frieze and of the ceiling which are dedicated to the cult of the heart.
The Electress Henriette Adelaide was inspired to adopt this

décor and the symbolic pictures (ascribed to Caspar Amort, 1669) by the novel "Clélie" (by Madeleine de Scudéry) which appeared in 1654, which also contained an allegorical map - similar to the "Love Map" reproduced on the rear wall.

Wood carvings

Johann Pader. Basic motif is the heart form; in addition tendril ornamentation with putti, monogram FM and HA (Elector Ferdinand Maria and his wife Henriette Adelaide); the eastern part replaced.

Principal pictures in the frieze:

Fireplace wall: Putto with map of the "love sections".

Entrance wall: Putto points to the "Friendship City" erected in the shape of a heart (with the Tower of Watchfulness, the Love Schools, the Armory of Confidentiality, the Temple of Love and the Prison of False Hearts). - Opposite: Three maids of honour of the Electress as the Three Fates (the Countesses Katharina Anastasia von Törring and Anna Maria von Törring-Seefeld and Countess Katharina Barbara von Spaur) embroider hearts in a tapestry, ascribed to Nikolaus Prugger, 1668/69. - In between and in the oriel, further symbols with hearts.

Ceiling paintings

In the middle: Swarms of putti hover over two hearts pierced by an arrow. - On the outside small pictures: Putti with hearts, allegorical figures with hearts and cartouches with the coats of arms of Bavaria and Savoy.

Marble fireplace

Fireplace panel (cast iron): c. 1730. - Mantelpiece mirror (stucco made to simulate marble with scagliola inlays), dated 1640 (in part reconstructed).

Furniture

Two guéridons (candlestick stands), Paris c. 1700.
Ebony veneer with marquetry of tortoise-shell, tin and brass. Gilt bronze fittings.

Small table, Paris c. 1700.
Marquetry of tortoise-shell and brass.

Folding table, probably South German; top c. 1710; base with silver appliqués, middle of the 17th century.
Top: Gilded copper sheet, with Alliance coat of arms of Hohenlohe and Hesse-Kassel or Hesse-Rheinfels-Rothenburg.

Two chairs, Munich c. 1720.

Painting

Style of Titian: Portrait of a Venetian Nobleman, Venice c. 1550.

Miniatures

Johann König: Orpheus and the Animals; Rome, 1613 (gouache).
Ebony frame with gold and lapis lazuli decor, Munich after 1613.

Unknown master: Elector Ferdinand Maria and his Wife Henriette Adelaide surrounded by their family, about 1672.
Water-colour and tempera on parchment.

Engelhard de Pee: Elisabeth, Wife of Duke Maximilian I of Bavaria, Munich c. 1600.

69 Green Chamber

The ceiling paintings (originally in the bedchamber of the Electress destroyed in 1944) by Antonio Triva (1673/74), the overdoors by Jacopo Amigoni and the gilded carved doors originate from the baroque room furnishings; ceiling replaced in 1958.

Ceiling paintings

Middle painting: "Fame of the Virtues of Henriette Adelaide". - Four corner paintings: "Wisdom" (with mirror), "Virtue" (with spear over vices), "Friendship" (with heart), "Fortitude" (with column).

Overdoors

Jacopo Amigoni: "Apollo and King Midas" and "Venus and Pan", c. 1720.

Tapestry

Allegory of Africa, signed at the bottom right Albert Auwercx, Brussels c. 1700, after a cartoon by Ludwig van Schoor.

Furniture

Two commodes, Munich c. 1725.
Veneer of palisander, gilt bronze fittings. - On top:

Clock on rocking pagoda, China, 18th century.
Blanc de Chine with colours of the "famille rose". Clockwork by Voisin, Paris.

Clock on elephant, China, early 18th century.
Bronze mounts Paris c. 1730, clockwork by Charles Voisin, Paris.

Two taborets, Munich about 1720.
Carved and gilded frames.

Paintings

German, early 18th century: Elector Max Emanuel of Bavaria, copy after Joseph Vivien, 1710.

Studio of Joseph Vivien, (after) 1722: Maria Amalia, wife of Hereditary Prince Karl Albrecht.

Probably German about 1700: Maria Anna Christina Victoria, eldest sister of Elector Max Emanuel, Dauphine of France.
Copy after a posthumous portrait of the princess, who died in 1690, painted by Joseph Vivien about 1700.

70 Connecting Room

Tapestries
Narrow wall: Diana and Endymion, probably Brussels c. 1690-1700.

Entrance wall: Mercury handing over the Infant Bacchus to the Nymphs of Nysa, probably Brussels c. 1690-1700.

Opposite: Triumphal Carriage of Bacchus with Ariadne, probably Brussels c. 1690-1700.

In the side room:

Paintings
Ferdinand IV, King of Hungary and Bohemia, son of Emperor Ferdinand III, after the original by Franz Luycx von Luxenstein, 1650/51.

Elector Johann Georg II of Saxony, after the original by Franz Luycx von Luxenstein, 1650/51.

Equestrian statue
King Louis XIV of France, Jean-Baptiste(?) Gobert, Paris 1695.
Bronze cast.

71 Golden Hall

The room which was newly decorated in 1666/67 with three windows facing the Residenzstrasse was originally an audience chamber of the Electress Henriette Adelaide. Only the ceiling pictures by Johann Heinrich Schönfeld from 1666/67 remain from the baroque room fittings. The frieze paintings by Caspar Amort are lost.

Ceiling paintings
In the middle: The Emperor Trajan accepts a Petition from a poor Woman in the Walachia. - On the outside, eight circular pictures: Princes of Foreign Nations give Audience and accept Petitions.

Tapestries
"Isaac dispatches Jacob to Mesopotamia" and "Jacob flees with his People and becomes reconciled with Laban", from a tapestry series of the History of Jacob, after cartoons by Michiel Coxie, woven in Brussels by Jan van Tieghem, about 1560/63 (On loan of the Bayerische Hypotheken- und Wechsel-Bank).

Paintings
German, between 1726 and 1729: Elector Karl Albrecht of Bavaria.

German, early 18th century: Princess from the House of Medici.

In the display cases
As an introduction to the treasures of the Silver Chambers which are exhibited in Rooms 100-103 (circular tour in the afternoon), silverware of the 16th and 17th century which does not belong to any of the services is displayed here.

On the narrow walls

Two display cases with court marshal staffs, whose silver pommels date to the 16th-18th centuries.

On the window piers:

German silverware of the 16th and 17th century:

First display case

Above: Oval dish, Johann Baptist I Weinold, Augsburg about 1645-50 - Beaker with cover, Jobst Zwickel, Augsburg about 1595-1600 - Beaker with cover of Duke Ferdinand of Bavaria, from St. Wolfgang in the Schwindach, Haag Country in Bavaria, Master PW, Munich 1601.

Below: Beaker with cover, probably Augsburg c. 1700 (from Würzburg) - Round dish with ostrich feather motifs in filigree, probably Augsburg, 17th century.

Second display case

Above: Tankard with cover and two tazzas, Balthasar Holweck, Nuremberg, early 17th century.

Below: Ewer and basin and two tazzas, Wolf Christoph Ritter, Nuremberg about 1630.

IN THE CIRCULAR TOUR II THE ROOMS 100-114 - (71-72) - 115-127 (Pages 158-200) FOLLOW HERE.

72 The Queen-Mother-Staircase

The western staircase to the main storey of the "Königsbau" (Royal Palace) erected in 1826-1835 by Leo von Klenze under King Ludwig I, originally led directly to the Queen's Chambers. The spiral flight of stairs is interrupted by a landing on the mezzanine; on the rear wall, marble statue of the wounded

Philoctet by Giacomo Spalla, Turin 1812. The flight of stairs ends on the upper floor with an estrade, which is closed towards the stairwell by paired Ionic marble columns. The vault of the stairwell is composed of a coffered semidome with stuccoed rosettes. After being damaged in World War II, the Queen-Mother-Staircase was restored in 1956-1958.

73 Passage to the "Königsbauhof" (Royal Palace Courtyard)

74 Vestibule

On the entrance wall, marble statue of Vesta by Canova's pupil Pietro Tenerani (1869).

75-79 Nibelungen Halls

The suite in the western ground floor of the Royal Palace comprises three large and two narrow halls and was designed after plans by Leo von Klenze in imitation of Italian models. The wall and ceiling paintings by Julius Schnorr von Carolsfeld are the first monumental representation of the medieval "Nibelungenlied" .

As in the upper storey of the "Königsbau" (Royal Palace), the epic was introduced here by order of King Ludwig I as subject of monumental painting. The paintings were executed in 1827-1834 and 1843-1867 with the assistance of Friedrich von Olivier and Wilhelm Hauschild (restored 1955-1960).

75 Hall of Heroes

The mural-portraits of the heroes of the epic are by Julius Schnorr von Carolsfeld; they are separated from each others by wall piers of stucco made to simulate marble.

Furnishings
Monumental vase in crater-shape of red marble with gilt bronze handles, about 1830/40.

White-blue tile stove, c. 1840.
Classicising ornamentation, in the upper part two lions and eagle.

76 Wedding Hall

On the walls between gilded stucco moldings, murals by Julius Schnorr von Carolsfeld of scenes from the first part of the "Nibelungenlied".

Furnishings
Two tables, Munich 1834/35.
Painted white and gold. - On top:

Four bronze craters, Munich(?) first half of the 19th century.

Bronze bust of Crown Prince Ludwig (later King Ludwig I), model by Bertel Thorwaldsen, Rome 1821, cast by Johann Baptist Stiglmaier, Munich 1824.

77 Hall of Treason   *Fig. 35*

On the walls between gilded stucco ornaments, murals by Julius Schnorr von Carolsfeld of the middle scenes from the "Nibelungenlied", i.e. from the Quarrel of the Queens in front of the Cathedral in Worms up to Siegfried's Death.

Furnishings
Two tables, Munich 1834/35.
White and gold painted frames. - On top:

Marble busts of King Maximilian II and his wife Marie, Johann Halbig, 1852 or 1855.

78 Hall of Vengeance

On the walls, between panels in stucco resembling marble, murals by Julius Schnorr von Carolsfeld, depicting the last part of the "Nibelungenlied", i.e. the Struggle and Decline of the Burgundians at the Court of King Etzel.

79 Hall of Lament

Murals by Julius Schnorr von Carolsfeld and William Hauschild framed by stucco moldings illustrate the Sorrow at the Decline of the Nibelungen.

80 Connecting Room

Sculptures
"Harmless" (called so from the beginning of the poem on the stone), Franz Jakob Schwanthaler, Munich 1803.
White marble. Originally erected in the English Garden near the Prinz-Karl-Palais (replaced there with a copy).

Portrait bust of Prince-Regent Luitpold, Wilhelm von Ruemann, 1901.
White marble.

81 Main stairs in the "Königsbau" (Royal Palace)

On the first landing of the stairwell:
Hercules and Atlas with the Vault of Heaven, Roman Anton Boos, Munich 1781.
From a group of statues with the deeds of Hercules which stood until 1944 in the northern Court Garden Arcades).

Exit to the large entrance hall of the "Königsbau".

CIRCULAR TOUR II

CIRCULAR TOUR II BEGINS WITH ROOMS 1-5 OF CIR-
CULAR TOUR I AND CONTINUES WITH ROOMS 82-99
DESCRIBED BELOW. - IT JOINS ROOMS 55-71 DESCRIBED
UNDER CIRCULAR TOUR I, CONTINUES IN ROOMS 100-
127 DESCRIBED BELOW AND ENDS WITH ROOMS 72-81
DESCRIBED IN CIRCULAR TOUR I.

82-88 Porcelain Chambers (European porcelain of the 18th century)

The Renaissance rooms of the Grotto Courtyard South Wing
were remodelled in 1730 by François Cuvilliés the Elder; the
furnishings of these "Yellow Rooms", the private apartment of
Elector Karl Albrecht, were lost in the 19th century. A second
grotto hall was located in the western Grotto Courtyard Wing
until about 1730, the marble columns of which can still be evi-
denced in the masonry on the window piers.

In addition to the table-service (see Rooms 100-103) kept in the
Silver Chambers, there were also collections of ceramic services, which initially contained only European earthenware and
East Asian porcelain (see Rooms 15-21) until the rediscovery
of porcelain in Meissen. The porcelain chambers here contain
European porcelain items of the 18th century; the European
porcelain stocks of the first half of the 19th century are exhibited instead on the main floor of the "Königsbau" (Rooms 14d-
14g).

82 First Porcelain Chamber

Meissen Manufactory

Entrance wall:

Early works in East Asian style, including peacocks with gilt bronze mounts, c. 1725.

Rear wall:

Left-hand display case, below: Tea-service with gilded strapwork decor and painted Chinese scenes, by Johann Gregor Hoeroldt, about 1723/24; gilded silver tray and stand, Augsburg work, by Johann Engelbrecht, about 1732/33. - Above: so-called Hunting Service with yellow ground and "Indian flowers" (Kakiemon decor), c. 1730-1735.

Middle display case, below: Four gilded tureens in East Asian style, c. 1725-1730, painted in Augsburg. - Above: Gilded tea-service with polychrome scattered flowers decoration, about 1745; set of vases with polychrome painted and modelled grapevine foliage, gilded masks and birds, c. 1725.

Right-hand display case, below: Tea-service with gilded strapwork decoration and painted Chinese scenes, by Johann Gregor Hoeroldt, 1723/1724; gilded silver tray and stand, Augsburg, by Johann Engelbrecht, c. 1732/33. - Above: Breakfast-service with yellow ground with painted harbour-scenes, c. 1730-1735.

Detached: Two flute vases with yellow ground with Chinese scenes in the style of Johann Gregor Hoeroldt (AR mark), c. 1730.

Exit wall:

Left-hand display case: Vanity set, c. 1735, made for Wilhelmine Amalie, widow of Emperor Joseph I.

Right-hand display case: Items from a dinner-service with sea-green ground, c. 1735.

Two chamber pots (pots de chambre), the upper one with Chinese scenes in gold painting, Meissen about 1730; the lower one Chinese export manufacture the European market, about 1700.

Detached display case:
Parts of a breakfast-service with gilded strap-work decoration, c. 1725-1735; the red genre scenes probably by the Augsburg painter Bartholomäus Seuter. - Figures and groups by Johann Joachim Kändler: Among others Cavalier and Lady at the Clavichord, soon after 1741; Lady with Fan, soon after 1736; Fox at the Piano, soon after 1743, in cooperation with Peter Reinicke, and Writing Cavalier, c. 1740.

Painting
Ferdinand Kobell (1740-1799): The Ford or "Morning".

83 Second porcelain chamber

Meissen Manufactory

Entrance wall:
Left-hand display case, above: Breakfast-service with painted and modelled scattered flowers and painted insects, c. 1740. - Two table candlesticks with shepherd and shepherdess, probably by Johann Joachim Kändler, c. 1750.

Right-hand display case: Figures by Johann Joachim Kändler and Johann Friedrich Eberlein, c. 1750; including Group of the Drunken Silenus, by J. J. Kändler, about 1766.

Rear wall:

Left-hand display case: Three birds (jay and two rollers), by J. J. Kändler, about 1740-1745. - Below: Large centre-piece, in the style of J. J. Kändler, probably c. 1760.

Right-hand display case: Three vases from the so-called "Snowball Set" by J. J. Kändler, c. 1740-1750.

Middle display case: Large scent vessel (pot pourri) with flower decoration, by J. J. Kändler, probably c. 1760.

Exit wall:

Left-hand display case: "Shepherding", by J. J. Kändler and J. F. Eberlein, c. 1750-1760.

Right-hand display case: Set of vases "Apollo" by J. J. Kändler, around 1760.

Window pier:

Above: Figures of Saints (painted), by J. J. Kändler and Peter Reinicke, between 1737 and 1744. - Below: Breakfast-service in "Royal Blue" for Duke Karl II August of Palatine-Zweibrücken, about 1775; painting after François Boucher in the style of Johann Georg Loehnig.

Detached display case:

"Judgment of Paris", by Johann Joachim Kändler or Michael Victor Acier, towards 1760.

Paintings

Marie Catherine de Silvestre: Pastel portraits of four children of Friedrich August II of Saxony (August III of Poland) and his wife Maria Josepha; from left to right: Albert, Maria Anna Sophie (later wife of Elector Max III Joseph of Bavaria), Maria Josepha and Maria Amalia Christina, 1740/1742.

137

Two landscapes by Ferdinand Kobell (1740-1799): "Noon" and "Evening".

84 Third Porcelain Chamber

Frankenthal Manufactory

Entrance wall:

Left-hand and right-hand display cases: Breakfast-service with painted rural scenes, by Johann Osterspey and Christian Winterstein, 1764. - Plates from the "Bird service", 1771. - Figures (including hunting group) by Johann Wilhelm Lanz, c. 1755-1760.

Rear wall:

Left-hand large display case: "Bird Service", 1771 with large cooler. - Figures by Johann Wilhelm Lanz.

Left-hand small display case: Rhinoceros as clock support, c. 1760, after a design by Peter Anton Verschaffelt. - Chinese figures by Johann Friedrich Lück, about 1760.

Large display case in the middle: "Toilet of Venus" by Johann Wilhelm Lanz, toward 1760 (the largest figural work of the Frankenthal production). - Middle: Set of vases with "Watteau Scenes", c. 1759/62.

Right-hand small display case: Figures by Konrad Link, about 1765 and Johann Friedrich Lück, about 1760.

Large display case at the right: "Bird Service", 1771, with centre-piece.

Exit wall:

Service from 1768 with scattered flowers in purple and gilded monogram EA (made for the Electress Elisabeth Auguste, the first wife of Karl Theodor). - Figures by Konrad Link: The

Three Graces and the Three Fates (allegory of the birth and death of the Hereditary Prince Franz Ludwig Joseph, son of Elector Karl Theodor and his wife Elisabeth Auguste), 1761; Meleager and Atalanta, about 1777; allegory of the recuperation of the Elector Karl Theodor (The Heeded Wishes of the Palatinate), 1775.

Window pier at the left:
Figure groups by Johann Friedrich Lück, about 1760 and Konrad Link.

Window pier at the right:
Figures by Carl Gottlieb Lück, about 1770 and Johann Friedrich Lück, about 1760.

First detached display case:
Below: Breakfast-service with Chinese scenes, 1764. - Chinese scenes and Chinese houses by Carl Gottlieb Lück, about 1770.

Second detached display case:
Below: "The Huntsman from the Electoral Palatinate" by Carl Gottlieb Lück, c. 1765-1772. - Figures by Konrad Link.

Paintings
Two marine pieces, Netherlandish, 18th century.

85 Fourth Porcelain Cabinet

Nymphenburg Manufactory

Entrance wall:
Items from two dinner-services, about 1760-1770.

Rear wall at the left:

Three large plates with floral painting, probably by Joseph Zächenberger, c. 1761/63. - Cavalier and two Ladies, perhaps by Johann Georg Härtel, c. 1750-1760. - Two "Indian Ducks", probably by Joseph Ponhauser, c. 1754/55.

Rear wall at the right:

Figures by Franz Anton Bustelli.

Above and middle: Putti as Ovidian divine Figures, c. 1775. - Turks drinking Coffee (subsequently combined from two Bustelli figures). - Cheese Vendor and Apple Vendor *(Fig. 24)*, about 1755. - Jealous Suitor, about 1761. - Below: Among others Bubble with Lady. - Hunting Picnic, about 1761.

Glass cupboard:

Munich, middle of the 18th century (attributed to Johann Michael Schmidt, in the style of François Cuvilliés); in it: Parts of a dinner-service, probably painted by Joseph Zächenberger, about 1761/63.

Painting

Studio of George Desmarées: Elector Max III Joseph, about 1750.

In contemporary carved frame with coats of arms of the four Bavarian tax districts.

86 Fifth Porcelain Chamber

Nymphenburg Manufactory

Wall display cases:

Items from the so-called "Pearl Service" by Dominicus Auliczek, 1792-1795.

Detached display case:
Figures by Franz Anton Bustelli (white).
Above: Figures from the Commedia dell'Arte: Harlequin, Captain, Colombine, Lucinde, Mezzetino, Pierrot, Lalagé and Isabella, c. 1760. - Below: Listener at the Well, Loving Couple in a Ruin, Lady with Book, Chinese Lady with Pineapple, Chinese Lad (from the Heathen Priest Group), several Putti.

Painting
Portrait of a Lady, French, about 1750.

87 Sixth Porcelain Chamber
French Manufactories

Entrance wall:
Dinner-service from the "La Reine" Manufactory, Paris c. 1775-1780.

Rear wall:
"Bird Service" from the Sèvres Manufactory, 1759.

Exit wall:
"Bird Service" from the "La Reine" Manufactory, Paris about 1775-1780.

First detached display case:
Below: Inkwell from the Sèvres Manufactory, about 1760/61. Biscuit figures from the Sèvres, La Courtille and Mennecy-Villeroy Manufactories. - Above: Tea-service from the Vincennes Manufactory (1753).

Second detached display case:
Below: Biscuit figures from the Sèvres, Mennecy-Villeroy and

La Courtille Manufactories. - Above: Coffee-service (with flowers and gold ornamentation), "La Reine" Manufactory, Paris c. 1775-1780.

Paintings
Franziska Christine von Pfalz-Sulzbach, c. 1730.

Portrait of a Princess from the Palatine-Neuburg Dynasty, German, about 1700.

88 Seventh Porcelain Chamber

German, French and English Manufactories

Opposite the entrance wall:
Large table-service from the "Duc d'Angoulême" Manufactory, c. 1790-1800.

Entrance wall:
Below: Höchst and Vienna Manufactories. - Middle: Vases and plates from the Frankenthal Manufactory, about 1780. - Above: Two lions with the coat of arms of the Salzburg Archbishop Sigmund III Christoph von Schrattenbach: Vienna Manufactory, about 1760/70. - Rural figure groups (including "Spring" and "Autumn"), Vienna Manufactory, by Anton Grassi, c. 1780.

Exit wall:
Left: Ludwigsburg, Vienna, Kassel, Fulda and Höchst Manufactories.
Middle: Works by the Vienna Manufactory, figures by Anton Grassi, c. 1780. Right: Höchst and Berlin Manufactories, and others.

Window wall:
Wedgwood (stoneware).

Paintings
Rape of Ganymede, 18th century copy after Correggio.

Exotic Birds, Netherlandish, 18th century.

89 Court Chapel   *Fig. 6*

The nave was erected in 1601-1603 inside the oldest part of the
Residence built by Maximilian I; ceiling stuccowork (with the
symbols of the Laurentian litany) 1614. The choir was not
added until 1630. In 1944 the choir and vault were heavily damaged and restored in 1956-1958.

High altar:
Overall design probably by Hans Krumper (about 1600); mensa
and altar-frame restored in 1958 after the original model. The
altarpiece (Assumption of the Blessed Virgin Mary) and the
painting above it (Holy Trinity) by Hans Werl, 1600.
The silver tabernacle with double-doors by Stephan Hoetzer
(Munich, probably after 1622).
Four reliquaries with silver fittings about 1610.
Four candelabra in gilded silver: Christoph Lencker, Augsburg,
about 1590-1595.
Antependium: Lampas lamé in the type of the so-called lace
pattern, probably France, early 18th century.
At the sides on the wall, two gilt bronze reliefs (holy water vessel with flat candlestick): Mary standing on the globe as Mother
of God and as Our Lady of Sorrows ("Pietà") by Guillielmus
de Groff, about 1726.

Choir:
Choir stalls (oak), probably Munich, about 1630.

The hanging eternal light, Johann Friedrich Canzler, Munich, about 1750.

Two heart urns for children of Elector Max IV Joseph (King Max I Joseph), Munich 1803 and 1821.

Side altars:

Design and execution (paintings and stuccowork) by Johann Baptist and Franz Zimmermann 1748; at the left St. Anna, at the right St. Maximilian. In front of each two large reliquaries, probably Munich about 1770.

At the left: Crucifix, South German, first half of the 17th century.

Organ

Munich around 1610.

On the lower balcony, with intact workings.

90 Lower landing of the Chapel Stairway

Tapestry

Tapestry from the so-called Grotesque Series consisting of twelve tapestries with Christian virtues, which were woven in the Munich Tapestry Manufactory under Hans van der Biest in 1604-1609 and 1613-1615 after designs by Peter Candid.

The tapestry in Room 90 was made between 1604 and 1609; Imperial Orbs of the Bavarian Imperial Archsewer dignity, embroidered (after) 1623.

Marble busts

Antique Head of a Roman Youth of the first century A.D. set into a Renaissance garmented bust.

Centaur head of the 18th century with garmented bust of the same date.

91-93 Sacred Vestments Rooms

The rooms belong to a part of the building erected by Maximilian I about 1600.

The ecclesiastical vestments and antependia displayed here come from the former Wittelsbach court churches, in particular from the Rich Chapel and the Old Court Chapel of the Munich Residence and from secularised monastery possessions.

Description clockwise, always starting at the left of the entrance

91 First Sacred Vestments Room

Vestments

Chasuble in chased velvet, Italy, early 17th century. - Embroidered amice of Anna Catharina Constanza of Poland, probably Germany or Italy, first quarter of the 17th century. - Chasuble and antependium, golden embroideries on dark red silk velvet using Osman embroideries, Munich probably 1620s. - Pearl mitre of the Mainz Elector-Archbishop Johann Karl Friedrich von Ostein, by Johann Sebastian Stein, Mainz, 1745. - Embroidered antependium with the Annunciation, probably Munich c. 1610/20. - Pearl mitre, probably Mainz, first half of the 17th century and by Peter Ehrlich, Mainz 1763. - Chasuble embroidered in petit-point with instruments of the passion, probably Munich c. 1610/20.

Marble busts

Two classicising Heads of Youths and one of a Girl (16th-19th centuries).

92 Second Sacred Vestments Room

Vestments

Antependium, needle painting in coloured silk on canvas over pattern sketch in dark brown ink, Italy or France, second half of the 17th century. - Chasuble in lampas, probably Italy, early 17th century. - Chasuble in ciselé violet velvet, probably Florence, early 17th century. - Antependium in lampas with Bavarian-Lorraines coat of arms, probably Italy, early 17th century. - Chasuble and antependium in ciselé green velvet, probably Florence, early 17th century.

Marble busts
Roman portrait head after Greek original of Alexander from the Tiberian-Claudian era set into a garmented bust of the 17th century.
Roman head of a Child (Geta), c. A.D. 200 set into a garmented bust of the 17th century.

93 Third Sacred Vestments Room

Vestments
Gold embroidered pluvial of the Polling vestments, probably Munich c. 1730/40. - Embroidered chasuble with "Indian" fruits and flowers, South Germany(?), first third of the 18th century. - Embroidered chasuble with coat of arms of the Electress Henriette Adelaide, probably Munich c. 1660/70. - Chasuble, Italy (Florence?), beginning of the 17th century. - Vestments with coat of arms of the Elector Johann Wilhelm of the Palatinate in green moiré, probably France about 1710. - Chasuble *(Fig. 28)* and dalmatic of the yellow Wessobrunn vestments, Munich 1749, donated by Maria Amalia, widow of Emperor Karl VII - Gold embroidered chasuble, dalmatic and mitre of the Polling vestments, probably Munich c. 1730/40.

Marble busts
Antonine portrait head after the Greek ideal sculpture of

Athena Ince dated from the end of the 5th century B.C. Roman portrait head of a Young Athlete with headband after a Greek original of the second-first century B.C. Head of a Roman Youth of the first century A.D.

Head of a Boy, Venice 16th century.

All heads set in garmented busts of the 16th-18th century.

94 Chapel Stairway

Tapestries

Three tapestries from the so-called Grotesque Series (see Room 90), woven at the order of Duke Maximilian I in the Munich Tapestry Manufactory under Hans van der Biest in 1613-1615 after designs by Peter Candid.

95 Reliquaries Chamber

Maximilian I united a collection of "sacred objects" in the "Secret Chamber Chapel" or "Rich Chapel" (Room 98) erected in 1607 in the Grotto Courtyard Tract. The artistic setting was in keeping with the precious nature of the relics (from the group of the Christian history of salvation and of the saints). Several of these reliquaries go as far back as the time of Maximilians's father Duke Wilhelm V; later generations augmented the collection.

1 *Standing cross:* Probably Munich, about 1590.

Ebony, enamelled gold, precious stones, pearls. Angel figure at the foot, early 15th century.

2 *Reliquary casket with tower-shaped top:* Probably German, c. 1750.

Rock crystal, gilded silver, wooden base.

3 *Panel-type reliquary:* Augsburg c. 1590, lower part and lateral mounts by Matthäus Walbaum, c. 1625.
Gilded silver, enamelled gold, precious stones, pearls, gold embroidery.

4 *Crown,* probably from a statue of the Blessed Virigin Mary, Stephan Hoetzer, Munich, c. 1630/40.
Gilded silver, gold, part enamelled, rock crystal, rubies, diamonds.

5-6 *Two reliquary pendants:* Italian, c. 1800-1810.
Gilded silver.

7 *Reliquary monstrance:* German, early 17th century.
Rock crystal, agate, chalcedony, gilded silver, pearls.

8 *Crucifix:* Munich c. 1610-1620.
Ebony, gilded cast silver, precious stones.

9 *Crucifix:* Munich c. 1590-1600.
Ebony, wax, precious stones, enamelled gold, ivory.

10 *Small niche altar with Loreto Madonna:* Probably Rome, second quarter of the 17th century.
Ebony, lapis lazuli, amethyst and agate and other precious stones, part gilded cast silver, enamelled gold, pearls.

11 *Reliquary casket:* Munich c. 1600.
Rock crystal, ebony, enamelled gold mounts, precious stones, pearls.

12 *Relic capsule:* Probably German, c. 1620.
Rock crystal, gilded silver, painted portrait.

13 *Tower-shaped reliquary:* Munich c. 1590-1600.
Ebony, enamelled gold mounts, precious stones, pearls, gold embroidery.

14 *Reliquary monstrance:* Munich c. 1740.
Enamelled gold, brilliants.

15 *Box reliquary with tower-shaped top:* Munich or Augsburg, c. 1580-1590.
Ebony, enamelled gold mounts, rubies, pearls, cut glass.

16 *Ivory relief "Resurrection of Christ":* Munich c. 1700.
Ivory, black stained wood, silver, precious stones. The frame by the Munich goldsmith Johann Baptist Rousseau, c. 1770. Counterpart to No. 33.

17 *Pendant with particle of the cross:* Rome, about 1716
Brilliants, emeralds, silver setting, gilded and enamelled in part.

17a *Base for reliquary monstrance No. 21:* Georg Jungmair, Augsburg about 1610.
Ebony, gilded and enamelled silver mounts.

18 *Panel-type reliquary:* Munich c. 1580-1590.
Ebony, enamelled gold mounts, pearl embroidery. Counterpart to No. 31.

19-20 *Two relics of the heads* of the Popes Eleutherius and Lucius with tiaras.
Crown bodies: Maximilian Ulrich Daumann, Munich 1754; appliqués: Augsburg end of the 16th century; pearl embroidery: By Franz Joseph Antoni Janssens, Munich 1754/55.

21 *Three-part reliquary monstrance:* Probably Augsburg 1590, closely allied to the studio of Abraham Lotter.
Embossed and cast silver, enamelled gold, precious stones, pearls. Design in the form of a Late Gothic monstrance. Figural scenes from the Passion (at the side), Appearance of Christ to Mary Magdalene (middle), Soldiers under the Cross (at the top), Pietà, surrounded by angels with the Instruments of the Passion (at the top), penitent Mary Magdalene (back); single figures: Melchisedeck, Moses, allegories of Virtues, Evangelists, Fathers of the Church, Peter and Paul and others.

22-23 *Two panel-type reliquaries:* Probably Munich towards 1600.
Ebony, enamelled gold mounts, onyx cameos, pearls.

24-25 *Two reliquaries in monstrance form:* Munich or Augsburg c. 1610.
Ebony, enamelled gold mounts, pearls.

26-27 *Two reliquary monstrances:* Probably Matthäus Walbaum, Augsburg c. 1600.
Ebony, part gilded silver, pearl embroidery.

28 *Reliquary:* Augsburg c. 1580.
Base and crowning capsule are later additions. Rock crystal, enamelled gold, gilded silver, carnelian, pearls and pearl embroidery.

29 *Tower-shaped reliquary:* Munich c. 1590
Gold, enamelled gold, rubies.

30 *Bust of St. Mauritius:* Christoph Angermair, Munich c. 1630.
Ivory, green jasper, ebony with gilded silver mounts.

31 *Panel-type reliquary:* Munich c. 1580-1590.
Ebony, enamelled gold mounts, pearl embroidery. Counterpart to No. 18.

32 *Relic capsule:* Italian, c. 1720-1730.
Gold, brilliants.

33 *Ivory relief "Ascension of the Blessed Virgin Mary":* Munich c. 1700.
Ivory, black stained wood, silver, precious stones. The frame by the Munich goldsmith Johann Baptist Rousseau, c. 1770. Counterpart to No. 16.

34 *Tower-shaped reliquary:* Stephan Hoetzer after a design by Hans Krumper, Munich 1622-1626.
Ebony, gilded cast silver, precious stones, use of Turkish mounts with turquoises.

35 *Crucifix:* Johannes I Lencker, Augsburg c. 1610.
Cast gold and chasing, enamelled in part, precious stones, olivewood.

36-37 *Two three-piece reliquary monstrances:* Gottfried Lang after a design by Hans Krumper, Munich 1626.
Gilded silver, enamelled gold, cut glass.

38-41 *Four reliquaries in tabernacle form:* Ulrich I Ment, Augsburg c. 1620-1630.
Gilded silver base, enamelled gold, cut glass.

42 *Pax (Instrumentum pacis):* Goldsmith work, Italy c. 1570, altered in Munich c. 1620; miniature paintings by Hans Werl, Munich 1592 after Hans von Aachen
Gilded cast silver, enamelled gold mounts, precious stones, onyx, onyx cameos, pearls.

43 *Tower-shaped reliquary:* Jeremias Michael, Augsburg c. 1610-1615.
Gilded silver, enamelled gold, precious stones, pearls; Crowning statuette: St. Ambrosius. Counterpart to No. 62.

44 *Table reliquary in altar form:* Gottfried Lang, Munich 1626.
Ebony, silver, enamelled gold, precious stones, rock crystal, pearls, gold embroidery on velvet.

45-46 *Two tower-shaped reliquaries:* Munich c. 1600, after a design by Hans Krumper.
Enamelled gold, precious stones, pearls. Crowning statuettes: St. Anna and St. Peter.

47-48 *Relics of the heads* of John the Baptist and his mother Elizabeth with floral crowns: Munich c. 1620; embroidery Franz Joseph Antoni Janssens, Munich 1754-1756.
Green velvet, silver embroidery, pearls, rubies, diamonds, gold enamel.

49-50 *Two reliquary monstrances:* Probably Melchior Mair, Augsburg c. 1610-1620.
Gilded silver, enamelled gold mounts. Supporting figures: St. Rupert and St. Korbinian.

51 *Table reliquary:* Stephan Hoetzer, Munich 1622-1626, using Turkish ornamental mounts in nephrite.
Cast silver part gilded, precious stones, cut glass, gold embroidery on velvet.

52-54 *Reliquary shrines with pyramidal reliquaries at the sides:* Munich 1624 *(Fig. 8).*
Ivory, precious stones, corals, gilded and enamelled silver mounts, cut glass, gold and pearl embroidery on velvet.

55-56 *Two tower-shaped reliquaries:* Probably Munich c. 1590
Gold partially enamelled, rubies, cut glass. Crowning statuettes: St. Walburga and St. Stephen.

57 *Three-part reliquary monstrance:* Georg Jungmair, Augsburg c. 1625.
Gilded silver, enamelled gold, precious stones, pearls. The node and the three cylindrical attachments probably Augsburg c. 1570.

58-59 *Two disc reliquaries in the form of monstrances:* Bernhard Peter, Munich 1619.
Gilded silver with enamel, precious stones, pearls.

60 *Panel-type reliquary:* About 1600
Chased and gilded silver, pearls and precious stones, rear with engraved Resurrection of Christ.

61 *Framed silver relief of the Carrying of the Cross with a holy water stoup:* Rome c. 1612/13
Ebony, chased cast silver, enamelled gold mounts, precious stones.

62 *Tower-shaped reliquary:* Jeremias Michael, Augsburg, c. 1610-1616.
Gilded silver, enamelled gold, precious stones, pearls. Crowning statuette: St. Martin. Counterpart to No. 43.

152

63-64 *Two monstrance reliquaries:* Probably Joseph Grossauer, Munich c. 1750.
Chased silverwork.

65-66 *Two monstrance reliquaries:* Andreas Dräxler, Munich c. 1730-1740.
Chased, part gilded silver.

67 *Holy water vessel in the form of an altar:* Giovanni Giardini, Rome 1709.
Gilt bronze, chased silver figures (Fides and Castitas), lapis lazuli.

68 *Pyramidal reliquary:* Probably German c. 1720.
Rock crystal, gilded silver setting.

69 *Monstrance reliquary:* Italian c. 1710-1720.
Rock crystal, gilded silver in filigree work.

70 *Pietà:* Italian c. 1770.
Cast silver, gilded copper, coral, precious stones.

71 *Panel-type reliquary:* Ignaz Franzowitz, Munich 1777.
Gilded silver, gold sequins, precious stones.

72 *Reliquary casket:* Hieronymus Priester, Augsburg c. 1670-1674.
Gilded and enamelled silver, agate, precious stones, pearls, gold sequins, velvet.

73 *Cross reliquary:* Cruciform upper part with engravings, towards 1500; shaft and base, South German c. 1760-1770.
Upper part: Gilded silver; shaft and base: Gilded copper; stone trimming and settings of the upper part, probably 18th century.

74 *Small tower-shaped reliquary:* South German c. 1720-1730.
Chased silverwork, glass.

In the detached display case:
Relic shrine, so-called "Kindlschrein", Munich, upper part 1611, lower part towards 1626
Ebony, gold, gold enamel, onyx cameos, precious stones, cut glass, gold embroidery on silk.

96 Gallery of the Court Chapel (Room 89)

Rear walls of the side gallery corridors:
36 miniature pictures of a "Hermit Series", probably German towards 1650.

97 Vestibule of the Rich Chapel

Portal of the Rich Chapel 1607 in stucco made to simulate marble, restored in 1960-1965.

Paintings
Above the portal: Peter Candid: The Annunciation, c. 1607.

After Christoph Schwarz: The Last Judgement, Munich c. 1600.

Glass painting
Upper Rhenish (Heidelberg), early 16th century, style of Hans Baldung Grien.

Silver statue
Mother of God in a mandorla, Ignaz Franzowitz, probably after designs by Hubert Gerhard, Munich towards 1600.
Cast silver work (counterpart in the Servite Convent in Innsbruck). Crown, mandorla and base are components from the time around 1780. Part gilded copper, silver mounts.

Tapestries
Two tapestries from the so-called Grotesque Series (see Room

90 and 94), woven in the Munich Tapestry Manufactory under Hans van der Biest between 1613 and 1615 after a design by Peter Candid.

98 Rich Chapel   *Fig. 7*

The private oratory of Maximilian I, in the middle of the western Grotto Courtyard Complex, was originally called the "Secret Chamber Chapel". Hans Krumper is regarded as the creator of the extremely richly decorated room. Consecration in 1607; by about 1615 the work was largely completed.

The Chapel was severely damaged in 1944. The vault collapsed, the remainder was gutted. However, the most important elements survived (main altar, ornate organ, cover of the reliquary shrine, numerous reliquaries and silver statuettes, as well as the glass windows of the dome and some scagliola works). The room structure was reconstructed from the ruins, and the quite considerable voids filled in and added to.

The ceiling opens up to the oval tambour with eight stained glass windows (original). The ceiling is decorated with gilded stucco decoration on a lapis lazuli-coloured ground (azurite): Tendrils and garlands with the initials ME (Maximilian and Elisabeth); these parts are mostly copies. The reliefs in terra cotta appearing in between were reconstituted from the preserved fragments; the missing sections were replaced. The depictions show: Life of the Virgin Mary, Apostles, Saints, Resurrection and Ascension of Christ.

The scagliola portal is a reconstruction. The gilded terra cotta Christ in the niche over the door, copied from the famous statue by Michelangelo in S. Maria sopra Minerva in Rome, is original, as are the two gilded terra cotta putti on the pediment.

The walls of the room are lined with stucco made to simulate reddish marble. Panels of the frame-sections with flower vases, tendrils and geometrical motifs by Blasius Pfeiffer (Fistulator).

155

They belong to the earliest decoration of the room and were reconstructed by means of remnants and photographs. In 1632, scagliola fields with flowers and scenes from the Life of the Virgin Mary (probably made by Wilhelm Pfeiffer-Fistulator) were added, of which - after the war destruction - only five on the window wall and one on the rear wall were preserved (the other panels were augmented or remade); the figural depictions are free copies after Dürer.

The floor is inlaid with multicoloured marbles and stones (including red variegated porphyry). In the middle: Amethyst rose.

Furnishings

Altar, c. 1605-1610.

Ebony case by Paulus Dietrich, Munich; silver ornamentation Augsburg, incorporating older parts, coming probably from a silver altar commissioned by Duke Albrecht V; main masters: Hans Schebel (c. 1565-1570) and Jakob Anthoni (c. 1605/06), on the burnt side altars formerly silver reliefs by Hans IV Pfleger (c. 1614).

On the ebony case silver ornamentation: Reliefs with biblical and allegorical depictions; also figural and ornamental relief-decoration on the mounts, frieze moldings, handles and figures fully in the round. In the middle, six-part high relief with depiction of the Crucifixion. In the pediment, oval relief with representation of God the Father.

In place of the burnt altars at the sides: Three panel-type reliquaries on each side, Augsburg c. 1600-1610.
Ebony with silver mounts.

Figures, silver-cast on ebony socles.
Salvator Mundi and Twelve Apostles (on the central altar and on the sides), attributed to Jakob Anthoni, Augsburg soon after 1600. - Four candlesticks held by standing putti (on the central

altar), Bernhard Peter, Munich c. 1615. - Four candlesticks held by kneeling angels (on the sides), Augsburg c. 1600. - Crucifixion group (at the left), Jakob Anthoni, Augsburg c. 1613/14. - Archangel Michael (at the right), Munich beginning of the 17th century (according to tradition, casting by Duke Maximilian I). - Christ with Cross-pennant (on the shrine), attributed to Georg Lang, Augsburg c. 1610-1620.

Reliquary shrine, Munich c. 1590.
Cut glass perhaps by Zacharias Peltzer after a design by Friedrich Sustris. Mounts for the most part from the beginning of the 17th century.

Ornate organ, Munich and Augsburg, end of the 16th/beginning of the 17th century.
Housing and decoration largely by the goldsmiths Jakob Melper(ger) and Hans Sepier and the turner Georg Haas, Munich c. 1614; older parts were incorporated into the ornate organ, such as the ivory plaques painted in the late 1580s by Joris Hoefnagel and the organ pipes crafted by the Augsburg goldsmith Jakob Schenauer c. 1590.

99 Antler Corridor

Antlers from Royal Bavarian possession inscribed with information on the hunter and the place where the deer was killed.

Engravings
Johann Elias Ridinger (1695-1767): Hunting scenes and animal pictures.

CIRCULAR TOUR II PROCEEDS FROM HERE INTO THE RICH ROOMS WHICH ARE ALSO ACCESSIBLE IN CIRCULAR TOUR I. - ROOMS 55-71 FOLLOW (PAGES 96-130).

100-103 Silver Chambers, former Council of State Chambers and "Hartschiersaal" (Bodyguards' Hall)

The baroque appointments of the halls together with the Papal Chambers (Room 66-71) and the "Hartschiersaal" (Bodyguards' Hall, Room 103) belonging to the suite of the Electress Henriette Adelaide were destroyed by fire in 1674. Under King Max I Joseph, they were given a simple Empire decoration, which was destroyed in 1944. Its earlier name derives from the meetings of the Bavarian Council of State, corresponding to the present Cabinet, held here until 1918 presided over by the King or the Prince Regent Luitpold (see the furniture in Room 14c).

In the 19th century, the treasures of the Silver Chambers were kept on the ground floor, in the present Sacred Vestments Rooms (Room 91-93). Until World War II they were displayed in Rooms 86-88 (now the Porcelain Chambers of the 18th century) on the Grotto Courtyard.

Since 1974, the enormous collection of the Wittelsbach table-silver still in the Munich Residence has been exhibited for the first time in its entirety in the former Council of State Chambers and the Bodyguards' Hall. The exhibited sets comprise around 3500 pieces.

Despite all the losses, the Silver Chambers of the Munich Residence together with those in London, Stockholm and St. Petersburg are among the most important in Europe. As early as in the mid-15th century, a separate silver tower in the "Neuveste" (prior to its razing in 1832, located in the north-eastern corner of the present Residence) was required to hold the silver collection. In 1558 "Silver Chamber Rules and Regulations" were formulated and in 1585 an inventory was compiled. In times of need, when the treasury was empty, stocks of the Silver Chambers were used - or its treasures were captured as booty: During the Thirty Years War, a part was robbed by the

Swedes in 1632; when in 1648, an attempt was made to flee with the rest on the river Inn to Braunau, the ship sank on the 8th of May near Mühldorf. The collection was once again decimated in 1706 when the Emperor Joseph I ordered the entire silver collection of Elector Max Emanuel (who had been driven out of Bavaria during the War of the Spanish Succession) to be melted down for new currency in Augsburg. In 1751 at the order of the Elector Max III Joseph, older stocks of silver were smelted. However the collection was also augmented through silver stocks brought by the Wittelsbachs from the Palatine dynastic lines: Max IV Joseph from the line Zweibrücken-Birkenfeld, for example, brought with him rich stocks of the "Zweibrücken Table Silver" with exquisite works by Strasbourg and Mannheim silversmiths (Johann Jacob Kirstein and Carl Ludwig Jung). However, as early as 1799 - the year when he succeeded to the title - he was forced to melt down half of the Silver Chambers stocks to replenish the War Treasury against Napoleon.

The stocks grew again with the acquisition of pieces from the treasuries of the secularized Prince-Bishoprics of Bamberg and Würzburg at the beginning of the 19th century. The Silver Chambers however received their greatest expansion through King Max I Joseph, who demonstrated his newly acquired royal title: In 1806, when he was elevated to the Kingship, he ordered a new set of table-silver from the Princely Öttingen-Wallerstein court jeweler Seethaler and Sohn in Augsburg and turned in old silver in exchange in order "to restore the due brilliance to the Silver Chamber". In 1816/17 the largest ever silver service of truly regal appearance was purchased from the same firm: The gilded "Parisian Silver", with 502 pieces, probably the largest and best preserved vermeil service of the Napoleonic Era; at the same time a smaller service of non-gilded silver was bought from Seethaler. Both services had been made around 1807-1809 by the court goldsmiths of Napoleon, Martin-Guillaume Biennais and Jean-Baptiste-Claude Odiot, in Paris for

Napoleon's youngest brother Jérôme, who had resided in Kassel since 1807 as King of Westphalia. After Jérôme's flight in 1813, the two series were auctioned in 1816 in Stuttgart, purchased there by Seethaler and sold in 1816/17 to the Munich court; Seethaler provided the service with the royal coat of arms of Max I Joseph.

100 First Silver Chamber

Paintings

Peter Jakob Horemans: Two portraits of the Electoral Silver Stewards Gall and Hölzl Munich 1772 and 1773.

Table display case on the entrance wall:

Gilded carving set (with coat of arms of Maximilian I), about 1600 - Cutlery with green-dyed stag-horn handles (with monogram of Elector Karl Theodor), Solingen 1747 - Two golden sets of cutlery, probably Augsburg about 1750 - Gilded silver cutlery, by Johann V Beckert and Abraham IV Warnberger, Augsburg 1753-1755 - Lark spits, 19th century.

Table display case on the exit wall:

Golden cutlery set of Prince-Bishop Adam Friedrich von Seinsheim with sun motive, probably Augsburg about 1770 (from Würzburg) - Two golden cutlery sets, probably Augsburg about 1750 - Gilt silver cutlery, by Johann V Beckert, Augsburg 1763-1765 (at the left) with spice-box by Peter Christian Roser, Augsburg 1769-71 - Golden cutlery set with spice-box, probably Augsburg middle of the 18th century (at the right) - Two gilt silver shells.

On the window piers:

Two cases with gilt silverware by Augsburg silversmiths of the 18th century.

Worthy of particular note are:

Left display case above: Ewer and basin, by Johann Jakob II Biller, Augsburg 1749-1751 - below: Ewer and basin, by Johann Jacob II Bruglocher, Augsburg 1740.

Right display case above: Ewer and basin, by Bernhard Heinrich Weyhe, Augsburg 1769-1771, with coat of arms of King Max I Joseph (from Bamberg) added later - below: Salver, by Abraham IV Drentwett, Augsburg 1769-1771, with coat of arms of King Max I Joseph added later - Gilt Ewer and basin, by Johann Jakob II Biller, Augsburg 1749-51.

Wall display cases:

Principally Augsburg and Munich works, with few exceptions, first half of the 18th century.

Worthy of particularly note are:

At the right: Rinsing vessel and "Mundkeller" (cooler) with coat of arms of the Elector Max Emanuel as Sovereign of the Spanish Netherlands, by Claude Ballin the Younger, Paris 1712/1713 ("Fermier" Florent Sollier) - Coffee-pot with coat of arms of the Elector Karl Albrecht, 1741 - Writing utensils, Bayonne 1720 (Maker's mark EP) - Two decagonal salvers with coat of arms of Elector Max Emanuel as Sovereign of the Spanish Netherlands, Paris 1714 ("Fermier" Florent Sollier).

Middle: Pint beaker with coat of arms of Elector Ferdinand Maria, Augsburg 1674, as well as quart beaker with coat of arms of Elector Max Emanuel, Johann Georg I Oxner, Munich 1690 and Master I.S. (Johann Strobel?) - Four oval tureens with cover, Philipp Jakob VI Drentwett, Augsburg 1749-51 - Six salvers with the Imperial Vicariate coat of arms of the Elector Karl Albrecht, Jakob II Bruglocher, Augsburg 1740.

At the left: "Mundkeller" (cooler) and wine-cooler with coat of arms of the Elector Max Emanuel of Bavaria, Johann Georg I Oxner, Munich 1715 - Helmet jug and bowl (with royal crown and date 1812 added later), Martin Müller or Martin Mitnacht, Augsburg 1732/33(?).

101 Second Silver Chamber

Augsburg and Strasbourg silver of the second half of the 18th century, including stocks of the Zweibrücken table silver of Max IV Joseph and of the Bamberg table silver of Prince-Bishop Adam Friedrich von Seinsheim.

Worthy of particular note are:

Window wall:

Table display case on the left: Cutlery sets, by Johann Jakob Kirstein, Strasbourg 1780-90 - above: Tureen or pot à oille (1713/14) and stand (1714/15) *(Fig. 29)* as well as beaker with cover (1713/14) in gilded silver with coat of arms and monogram of Elector Max Emanuel as Sovereign of the Spanish Netherlands, Paris 1713-1715 ("Fermier" Florent Sollier).

Left pier display case above: Small bowl with cover (Ecuelle), Paris about 1730 - Small tureen and ewer and basin, by Johann Ludwig Imlin the Younger, Strasbourg c. 1720-30 and 1728 respectively - below: Three gilt salvers by Abraham IV Drentwett, Augsburg 1769-1771 (from Bamberg).

Right pier display case below: Three gilt salvers by Daniel I Schäffler, Augsburg 1719/20.

Table display case at the right: Among other things dessert-cutlery, by Martin-Guillaume Biennais, Paris beginning of the 19th century.

In the case above: Powder-box, two candlesticks, tureen with stand and spice-box and cutlery, Johann Jacob Kirstein, Strasbourg 1786.

Made for Auguste Wilhelmine of Palatine-Zweibrücken on the occasion of the birth of her first son Ludwig, later King Ludwig I. - In 1796 the necessaire came into the possession of Caroline of Baden, the second wife of the later Bavarian King Max I. Joseph. At that time the alliance coat of arms was affixed to the pieces. (Except for the powder-box and the candle-holder, all on loan from the Bayerische Landesbank, Girozentrale).

Wall display cases:

At the right: Large fish platter with monogram of the Elector Karl Theodor, (before) 1773 - Two ewers and basins, by Johann Jakob II Biller, Augsburg 1749-1751 - Two tureens, by Johann Jakob Bruglocher, Augsburg 1739-1741 - Three silver bowls with blue glass liners ("Cooler"), by Johann Andreas Dressel, Augsburg 1787-1789.

Middle: Parts of the Palatine-Zweibrücken table silver of Max IV Joseph, by Johann Jacob Kirstein, Strasbourg 1780-1790 and candelabra, by Carl Ludwig Jung, Mannheim 1790-1793 - Two small tureens of the Augsburg masters Johann Wilhelm Damman 1769-1771 and Carl Samuel Bettkober 1769-1771 *(Fig. 30)* - Four ewers and basins, by Adolf Carl Holm, Augsburg 1769-1771 - Chocolate-pot with Zweibrücken coat of arms (below, at the left middle), by Adelhard von Hundel, Mannheim about 1742-1753 - Chocolate-pot with Zweibrücken coat of arms (below, left corner), by Musculus, Mannheim(?) middle of the 18th century.

At the left: Two ewers and basins by Johann Jakob II Biller, Augsburg 1749-1751 - Tea-kettle with rechaud (stand and burner), by Johann Christoph Engelbrecht, Augsburg 1755-1757.

102 Third Silver Chamber

Painting

Domenico Quaglio: View of the so-called Cabinet Garden of the Munich Residence (with the Neptune statue by Georg

Petel, today in Room 43), before erection of the "Königsbau" (Royal Palace) 1826.

Munich and Augsburg table silver, for the most part additions to the table silver of King Max I Joseph, first half of the 19th century. The turning point in the style of the table silver caused by the influence of the Parisian models for the Empire oriented towards antiquity is very apparent.

Worth special attention:

Window wall:

Display cases on the sides: Pieces from the table silver of Max I Joseph: Eight candelabra and two sauce-boats made by the firm Joseph Anton Seethaler & Sohn in Augsburg, 1807 - Four entremets dishes, by Marie-Joseph-Gabriel Genu, Paris c. 1807 - Four dishes with covers by Johann Georg Christoph Neuss, Augsburg 1817 - Plates, Munich 1827 and 1833.

Middle display case: Two candelabra made by the firm Joseph Anton Seethaler & Sohn in Augsburg, 1807 - Samovar by Gustav Friedrich Gerich, Augsburg 1793-1795 - Bedpan of Charlotte Auguste, daughter of King Max I, about 1810.

Wall display cases:

Upper row: Table candelabra by Anton Weishaupt, Munich 1822 - In the middle: Two table candelabra, by Martin-Guillaume Biennais, Paris c. 1807, and deep bowl with handles, by Anton Weishaupt, Munich c. 1820 - At the sides: Two sauce-boats, Anton Weishaupt, Munich 1826; eight sauce-boats by Max Carl Weishaupt, Munich 1866; Hors d'oeuvres dishes by Carl and Max Weishaupt, Munich 1830-1840.

Middle row (from the right): Tureens with liners and entremets dishes by Anton Weishaupt, Munich 1828 - From the same company entremets dishes with saucers 1833 and table candelabra 1820 - In the middle two coffe-pots, by Anton Weishaupt,

164

Munich 1818-1824 - Two large tureens with liners, by Carl and Max Weishaupt, Munich 1830-1840 - Six table candelabra by Anton Weishaupt, Munich c. 1820.

Lower row: Food covers by Anton Weishaupt and Louis Wollenweber, Munich 1828 and 1834.

103 Bodyguards' Hall

Named after the Electoral Bodyguards.

Tapestries

Five tapestries from the so-called Grotesque Series (see Room 90, 94 and 97), woven after designs by Peter Candid in the Munich Gobelin Manufactory under Hans van der Biest, 1604-1609 (tapestries on the narrow sides) and 1613-1615 (tapestries on the long wall).

Chandeliers

Three chandeliers, delivered by Larnaz Tribout, Paris c. 1833-1835, after a design by Leo von Klenze.

Bronze, silverplated and gilded. The chandeliers come from the so-called Dining or Flower Room, which used to be in the second upper story of the "Königsbau" (Royal Palace).

Display cases on the window wall:

Items from the silver banquet-service of the Parisian goldsmith Martin-Guillaume Biennais (Imperial Court Goldsmith of Napoleon); the serviece was originally made for King Jérôme of Westphalia and then purchased by Max I Joseph in 1816/17. The Service was supplemented with replicas by the Munich goldsmiths Anton and Carl Weishaupt, Zahn, Wollenweber and Seitz, who copied the silver service of Biennais and the vermeil service of Biennais and Odiot. (See the large display case). Worthy of particular note are:

In the two left-hand display cases: Food covers by Anton Weishaupt, Munich 1821-1822, the models for which were created by Martin-Guillaume Biennais in Paris about 1807 (penultimate and last case at the right) - Tureens with modelled group as knob of cover (Vertumnus and Pomona), by Martin-Guillaume Biennais, Paris about 1807, and their copies, by Anton Weishaupt, Munich 1821-1822 - Flat plates, some of them by Martin-Guillaume Biennais, Paris c. 1807 - Food covers by the Munich firm Zahn and Wollenweber, 1833 - Entremets dishes and carafe coasters, by Anton Weishaupt, Munich about 1824-1825 after a model by Jean-Baptiste-Claude Odiot, Paris about 1807 (penultimate and last case at the right).

Middle display case: Large vase with pierce-work body by Anton Weishaupt, Munich 1830, in the medallions, Apollo, Bacchant and three Muses - Two tea-kettles with rechaud (stand and burner), at the left by Johann Alois Seethaler and Georg Christoph Temmler, Augsburg 1811, at the right by Anton Weishaupt, Munich c. 1810-1820 - Goblet with cover and stand, first prize for the crossbow contest in Augsburg on August 1, 1824, by Johann Georg Christoph Neuss, Augsburg 1824.

In the last two display cases at the right: Food covers, dishes, carafe coasters, tureens with knobbed covers (Vertumnus and Pomona), Paris c. 1807, mostly by Martin-Guillaume Biennais.

Large detached display case:

Vermeil service (gilded silver) of King Max I Joseph, by Martin-Guillaume Biennais and Jean-Baptiste-Claude Odiot, Paris c. 1807-1809, originally made for King Jérôme of Westphalia, purchased in 1816/17 through the Augsburg silver-dealer Johann Alois Seethaler, consisting of 502 pieces.

The centre-piece of gilt-bronze, probably made in Munich about 1820, was acquired in 1972.

104-109 "Steinzimmer" (Stone Rooms)
(originally Imperial Chambers)   *Fig. 5*

The suite in the western wing of the Imperial Courtyard - originally intended as an apartment for state guests - was erected
at about the same time as the Treves Rooms (Rooms 46-53)
(1614, construction of fabric; 1616, furnishing completed).
However the consistent implementation of the enfilade is missing here, as is the strict symmetry of the ground-plan in the
alternation of the room dimensions. Like its (smaller and less
grand) counterpart in the Treves Rooms, the corridor - here
called Theatiner Corridor - does not run along the courtyard.
Rather it follows the course of the former Schwabinger Gasse
(Residenzstrasse), and thus deviates from the exact square
ground-plan. The resulting spandrels are filled by a stairwell
(Hans-Steininger Stairs) and several auxiliary rooms.

The name "Steinzimmer" (Stone Rooms) comes from the
stonework decoration in the rooms – with marble, stucco marble and scagliola. The pictorial programme of the Stone Rooms
is dedicated to the earthly and heavenly philosophy of Maximilian I, who allegedly also lived in these rooms. The sequence
of the themes, starting from the north is: The "Room of the
Elements" which illustrates the basic substances of the earth,
from which, as the "Room of the World" explains living creatures develop; these are - as is shown in the "Room of the Seasons" - subject to the annual cycle; in the "Room of Eternity"
the pictures point to metaphysical spheres, which find their
structure and clarification in the "Room of Religion" and in the
"Room of the Church".

Peter Candid and his assistants executed the paintings from
1614 to 1616; very few of these survived the Residence fire of
1674. Elector Max Emanuel ordered a restoration of the picture cycle, which was carried out from 1694 to 1698 by Giovanni Trubillio, Johann Anton Gumpp, Martin Moser and

Francesco Rosa. The cabinet-makers Georg Wohlgemut, Hans Neumayr and Peter Hörl created the coffered frames in 1694. Parts of the stuccowork, the portal and mantelpiece super-structures were also partially restored and supplemented by 1700. Additional minor changes (particularly on the fireplace walls) were made in the period 1799/1800. About 1890, the suite now serving as the apartment of the Prince Regent Luitpold was provided with parquet floors. In 1944 the rooms were severely damaged: All the central paintings of the wooden ceilings and their coffered frames were destroyed. By 1973 the preserved fragments had been reassembled. Copies of the earlier paintings were placed in the "Room of the Seasons". All of the wooden coffered ceilings are new, but have been reconstructed from the old models. Those paintings which survived were rehung, while the stuccowork (incorporating older remnants) has been restored, the door-frames and mantelpiece super-structures supplemented, remnants of the parquet flooring removed and the marble one restored. All doors, inlay work in walnut, ebony, letterwood and maple remained intact. A major part of the fittings also survived: Panel pictures, small bronzes, magnificent cycles of woven tapestries and splendid furniture from the time of Maximilian I (1598-1651), Ferdinand Maria (1651-1679) and Max Emanuel (1679-1726). The seating furniture comes for the most part - except for the throne chair in Room 109 - from the period about 1700/20 (coverings replaced).

104 Room of the Church

The door-frames and the fireplace niche (1614/16) of stucco simulating marble with scagliola panels as well as the part gilded stucco frieze have been restored with new additions. The scagliola panels above the door-frames are from the 18th century. The ceiling formerly showed an allegory of the Catholic

Church in the midst of the four continents. Only two of the paintings are preserved: Putti with Flowers by Francesco Rosa, 1695/1698. The frames of the picture panels were restored from the original designs.

Tapestries

From the so-called Artemisia Series, woven in the Royal Manufactory "des Gobelins" under Frans von den Planken and Marc de Comans after illustrations by Antoine Caron and designs by Henri Lerambert, Paris before 1612.

The series was acquired in 1612 by Maximilian I for the Residence in Munich. The tapestries bear the manufactory's mark and the Paris city mark. Material: Wool, silk, silver thread.

The subject is based on a allegorical story by Nicolas Houel. It tells of the Lycian Queen Artemisia, who ruled as regent for her son after the death of her husband Mausolos. These characters refer to the young successor to the French throne, the later Louis XIII and his mother Maria de´ Medici.

Entrance wall: Jurisdiction.

Fireplace wall: The Message - Instruction.

Exit wall: Coronation.

On the window pier: Woven cloth with coat of arms of Princess Anna Catharina Constanza of Poland, wife of Duke Philipp Wilhelm of Palatine-Neuburg, Brussels(?) c. 1630/40.

Sculpture

On the mantelpiece: Bronze bust of Elector Maximilian I, Alessandro Abondio or Balthasar Ableithner, Munich after 1640.

Mantelpiece panel

Cast-iron relief of the Electoral Bavarian coat of arms, about 1730.

Furniture

Desk with upright backpiece, Antwerp c. 1700.

Palisander with "Boulle" work (tortoise-shell, brass, tin, mother-of-pearl), gilded carving, including monogram of Elector Max Emanuel.

105 Room of Religion

Door-frames (early 17th century; upper part 18th century) and fireplace structure (1614/16) as well as part gilded stucco frieze (early 17th century) supplemented and restored. The pictorial programme of the ceiling was devoted to the Triumph of the Christian Religion - the subject of the (destroyed) central one, painted by Francesco Rosa from 1695 to 1698. The preserved side pictures depict allegories of truth, vigilance, patience and the power of religion. Putti carry liturgical objects for celebrating the mass. These paintings are by Christian Steinmüller, 1612. The picture-frames have been renewed.

Tapestries
from the so-called Artemisia Series (see Room 104).
Entrance wall: The Proclamation.
Exit wall: The Consul.

Painting
On the fireplace wall: Victoria (Victory) and Minerva, Johann Ulrich Loth, Munich 1636(?).

Memorial tablet
to Prince Regent Luitpold, who resided in the Stone Rooms and died in this room on December 12, 1912.

Bronzes
Samson and Delilah, Munich(?), perhaps second half of the 17th century.
After a statue by Hubert Gerhard (c. 1590).

Raging Hercules, Munich c. 1600, School of Hubert Gerhard.

On the mantelpiece:

Clock, David Buschmann, Augsburg about 1670-80.
Case veneered with tortoise-shell and decorated with modelled enamel.

Fireplace panel

Cast iron, combination of four relief scenes, 16th century.

Furniture

State table, probably Florence c. 1590.
Top: Marble and semi-precious stone inlay work (pietra dura). The supporting frame formerly richly decorated with ivory carving (by Christoph Angermair c. 1625/26) was destroyed in 1944; it has been replaced with a simple form.

106 Room of Eternity

Door-frames (with upper part from the 18th century) and fireplace structure (aedicule in the niche panel, c. 1800) reconstructed from the original parts and modern additions. This is also true for the stucco frieze. The central painting, destroyed in 1944, painted by Martin Moser in 1695/96, showed the allegory of eternity. The four side pictures painted by the same artist show emblems of eternity. The four tondi depicting illusionistic scenes are by Giovanni Trubillio (1697).

Tapestries

From a series of scenes from the Old Testament (Abraham Cycle), perhaps Manufactory of Willem Pannemaker, after design by Barent van Orley (died 1542), Brussels (city mark), third quarter of the 16th century.
Wool, silk, gold and silver threads.
Entrance wall: Abraham's Hospitality.
Exit wall: Rebecca at the Well.

Paintings

Two allegorical representations, Salus publica (public welfare)

and Closing of the Janus Temple as symbol of peace, Peter Candid, Munich probably 1615/20.
Cf. original location in Room 51 and 49.

Marble sculpture (over the mantelpiece)
Cupid, Peter Anton Verschaffelt, Mannheim c. 1770.

Bronzes
Allegory (Old Age?), Rome, end of the 16th century.
In the style of Guglielmo della Porta.

Venus after Bathing, early work of Hubert Gerhard, Munich c. 1590.

Fireplace panel
Cast iron with Electoral Bavarian coat of arms, c. 1730.

Furniture
Two chairs, c. 1720.
Covers renewed.

107 Room of the Seasons

The stucco ceiling survived the fire of 1674, but was destroyed in 1944. Restored after the original model. The paintings - Allegory of the Year (Annus) in the centre, Allegories of the Four Seasons each with a sign of the zodiac in the four corners and the remaining eight signs of the zodiac on the edge - were restored to their pre-1944 condition: The central picture and the allegories of spring and autumn, school of Peter Candid 1614/16, date from the original decoration having survived the fire of 1674. The others are copies of 1694/98 by Giovanni Trubillio. The early 17th-century door-frames with 18th century additions, have been restored. The fireplace is substantially original, and was after 1635 (with monogram MA, i.e. Maximilian I and his second wife Maria Anna of Austria). Fireplace wall redesigned at the end of the 18th century and restored in 1973.

Tapestries

From the series "The Deeds of the Palatine Count Otto von Wittelsbach" after cartoons by Peter Candid, woven between 1604 and 1611 in the Munich Gobelin Manufactory under Hans van der Biest.

Munich city mark and weaver´s mark. Wool, silk, silver and gold threads. - Borders with trophy decoration and monogram of Maximilian I and Elisabeth of Lorraine as well as alliance coat of arms Bavaria-Lorraine. In the lower border lettered cartouche with Latin explanation of the scenes. The richest production of the series hangs in the Stone Rooms; two simpler repetitions of the series are housed in the Germanic National Museum in Nuremberg and a complete but plainer duplication by the Parisian Manufactory of Frans van den Planken and Marc de Comans in Burg Trausnitz ob Landshut.

Entrance wall: Emperor Friedrich Barbarossa invests Otto with the Duchy of Bavaria in 1180 (c. 1609-1611).

Exit wall: Otto von Wittelsbach rescues the Imperial Army in the Veronese Gorge in 1155 (c. 1609).

Stone sculptures

Over the mantelpiece: Marble relief of Mars, Venus and Cupid. Antonio Lombardo, North Italy about 1505.

In the niches above the mantelpiece and the doors: Two busts of boys and a putto bust in marble, probably 17th-19th century; also two busts of the sons of the "Laocoon", 18th century.

Bronzes

Window wall: Head of an Emperor (fragment), Munich, recently ascribed to Hans Krumper, first quarter of the 17th century.

Chimney wall: Nessus ravishes Deianeira, Munich(?), second half of the 17th century.

After a group by Giovanni Bologna and Antonio Susini.

Hercules relieves Atlas, Munich(?), perhaps second half of the 17th century.
After a Flemish original from 1620-1630.

Fireplace panel
Cast iron, with the Electoral Bavarian coat of arms, c. 1730.

Furniture
Ornate table with octagonal scagliola top and carved supporting frame in walnut. The scagliola top (with monograms and coats of arms of Elector Maximilian I and his first wife Elisabeth of Lorraine): By Wilhelm Pfeiffer (Fistulator), Munich 1625/30.

Four chairs, about 1720.
Covers renewed.

108 Room of the World

Door-frames (scagliola tympanum 18th century) and mantelpiece (1614/16) have been restored. Stucco frieze from 1696 by Niccolo Perti, with figural reliefs (Triton, Thetis) on the window side, likewise restored. The ceiling pictures by Johann Anton Gumpp (1695/97) show putti with birds and various domestic and wild beasts of the earth, the air and the water from all continents as well as fabulous creatures. The central picture "Man as Ruler of the World" is lost. Wooden ceiling renewed.

Tapestries
from the series "The Deeds of the Palatine Count Otto von Wittelsbach" (see Room 107).
Entrance wall: Otto as Negotiator of Emperor Friedrich Barbarossa before Pope Hadrian IV in 1159 (c. 1609/10).
Fireplace wall: Otto forces Ferrara to surrender Hostages in 1158 (c. 1610). -

Otto marries Agnes von Wasserburg (more correctly Agnes Countess of Looz) (1609).
Exit wall: Otto as Founder and Builder of Landshut as Ducal City in 1182 (dated 1611) *(Fig. 15)*.

Woven tablecloth, Brussels, about 1660/70.

Bronzes
Hercules with the Nemean Lion (formerly fountain figure), south Netherlandish, c. 1630.

Silenus with the Infant Bacchus boy, Florence, c. 1700.

The Victor, perhaps Vincenzo Danti or Pierino da Vinci, Florence, mid-16th century.
Bronze statuette after the marble group of Michelangelo in the Palazzo Vecchio in Florence.

Vulcan, Munich(?) second half of the 17th century.
After the statue of an unknown Italo-Flemish master of the early 17th century.

On the mantelpiece: Farnese Hercules, probably France, c. 1700.

Fireplace panel:
Cast iron with Electoral Bavarian coat of arms, dated 1732.

Furnishings
On the window pier: Parts of the rear wall of a canopy. Fabric probably Italy, early 17th century; embroidery perhaps Munich, early 17th century.
Lampas with fine gold and silver filament and silver threads with nap effects (Bouclé). Gold and silver embroidery on blue silk velvet.

Ornate clock, silver chasing (with ruby glass and coloured glass), Augsburg c. 1690-1698. *(Fig. 11)*.

Silver case, ornaments and figures: Friedrich I Schwestermüller, Peter Winter and Michael I Heckel. Silver reliefs: Johann Andreas Thelott. Clockwork: Johann Christoph Schöner (signed). Base frame (wood, carved, gilded and silverplated): Heinrich Eichler(?).

Four chairs, c. 1720.
Covers renewed.

109 Room of the Elements

Door-frames (with scagliola of the 18th century in the tympanum) and fireplace niche (1614/16) restored. Stucco frieze from the building period and its mythological decorations on the window wall (by Niccolo Perti in 1696), for the most part renewed. Coffered ceiling with modern additions. The paintings by Giovanni Trubillio (1695/97) show allegories of the elements (Neptune for water, Cybele for earth, Vulcan for fire, Juno for air), depictions of the four winds and the four seasons. The central picture, the mourning Pan, was destroyed in 1944. In the corners, four emblems (the four elements).

Tapestries
from the series "The Deeds of Palatine Count Otto von Wittelsbach" (see Rooms 107 - 108).
Entrance wall: Otto receives in 1158 (not in 1153 as given on the tapestry) a Greek Legation in the Emperor's Name (1612-1614).
Fireplace wall: Homage of the Bavarian Estates (dated 1611). - Otto defeats Henry the Lion in 1180 (c. 1609/10).
North wall: Otto besieges Milan in 1158 (completed in 1609).

Bronzes
Two firedogs, Italy (Venice), early 17th century, in the style of Tiziano Aspetti.

Fireplace panel
Iron panel with Electoral Bavarian coat of arms, dated 1732.

176

Furnishings

On the window pier: Canopy for Maximilian I and Elisabeth; fabric probably from Italy, early 17th century; embroidery, Munich about 1610-1615.

Lampas with fine silver filament and silver threads with nap effects (Bouclé). Gold and silver embroidery; the Imperial Orbs appliquéd later (probably in 1623).

Throne, North Italy, early 17th century.
Walnut. Covering like that of the canopy in Room 108.

Carpet, Persia (Kaschan), early 17th century.

Two chairs, about 1700.
Covers renewed.

110-112 Four White Horses Hall, Imperial Hall, Imperial Staircase

The wing closing the Imperial Courtyard in the north accommodates the entrance and reception rooms of the entire complex: The Four-Shaft Hall (today vestibule of the Egyptian State Collection) located on the middle axis of the ground floor joins the Imperial Staircase, which leads up to the first upper storey and thus forms the entrance to the Imperial Hall and the adjoining Four White Horses Hall. Also the suites of the Stone and Treves Rooms were accessible from the North Wing. It was regarded as a festive and stately prelude as can be seen from earlier descriptions of the Residence. The Northern Wing along with the Western and the Eastern Wing was erected from 1612 to 1616 by Heinrich Schön and Hans Krumper; Peter Candid was responsible for the painting and tapestry decoration.

Shortly after his accession in 1799, Elector Max IV Joseph had the Imperial and Four White Horses Halls remodelled into living quarters of the so-called Court Garden Rooms for himself and his wife Karoline. The older structures in terms of size and appointments no longer satisfied contemporary taste and were scarcely used. The architect Charles-Pierre Puille, while largely retaining the enclosing walls of the Maximilian rooms, inserted partitions and a false ceiling in the Imperial Hall, in order to create rooms in the main floor and on the mezzanine. In addition, the number of window axes on the court garden side was increased, in order to obtain a window division more suited to the more numerous if smaller new Court Garden Rooms.

In 1944, the Court Garden Rooms were largely destroyed, together with their wooden panelling of 1799. However, most of the moveable furnishings and furniture was rescued. These items were displayed in 1966 in the south-eastern section of the Charlotte Chambers (Rooms 33-36). - Since an authentic restoration of the Court Garden Rooms on the original site - the northern side of the Imperial Hall - did not appear to be possible, it was decided to reconstruct the Imperial and Four White Horses Halls of the Maximilianic period. Residence drawings and descriptions of the 17th and 18th century served as a basis, as did various fragments - such as areas of the original stucco decoration - which, covered over by the 1799 alterations were rediscovered as a result of the war-damage. The restoration was further aided by the fact that many of the paintings and tapestries, which had originally decorated the Imperial and Four White Horses Halls, were still intact, having been placed in storage in 1799. The Imperial Staircase, which had not been affected by the remodelling of 1799, but which had been greatly destroyed in 1944, was also restored. The reconstruction work was completed in 1985. Consequently not only have three important rooms of the South German Late Renaissance been regained, but also important works of art have been restored to their original setting and made accessible to the public for the first time in almost two hundred years.

110 Four White Horses Hall

The Four White Horses Hall - so-called because of the four horses which pulled Apollo's sun chariot, the subject of the (lost) central picture - was severely damaged by the Residence fire in 1674. All of the ceiling panel-paintings, bar two, from the Maximilianesque decorations of 1614/15 were burnt. It was only in 1690-1694 that Elector Max Emanuel had the hall restored and the ceiling paintings remade in close imitation of the early 17th century programme. - During the later remodelling of the Four White Horses Hall in 1799, the room was shortened by several metres on the west side by the insertion of a narrow staircase. From 1980 to 1985 the room was reconstructed but the staircase was left in place, which means that rather than the original, slightly rectangular ground-plan, the Four White Horses Hall now has a square one. It also meant that two of the six large planet paintings surrounding the central one had to be left out.

Ceiling paintings

Originally, the ceiling was decorated with seven main pictures representing the planets, to which it was believed the sun and moon also belonged. The lost central picture by Francesco Rosa related to the sun and showed Apollo on the sun chariot drawn by four white horses. In the four, smaller circular picture-frames were representations of the four times of day (now lost) thematically related to the central painting. The planets personificated by divinities are grouped around the cental painting (beginning at the entrance in clockwise direction): Realm of Mercury by Johann Anton Gumpp; Realm of Venus and Realm of Jupiter by Johann Andreas Wolff; Realm of Diana by Francesco Rosa. - Small round pictures in the corners at the left: Three Graces and Saturn (reference to science and the arts as expressions of the human spirit and of the regulation of time), each by Francesco Rosa, 1692/1694; at the right: Ceres, Bacchus and Pomona (fertility of the earth, embodied in the three divinities, symbolizing grain, wine and fruit) as well as Justice, Law and Peace (Order of Human Society), each from the atelier of Peter Candid, 1614/15 (the only paintings preserved from the Maximilianesque Era, restored by Caspar Amort after the Residence fire).

The ceiling programme of the Four White Horses Hall shows the determining influence of the cosmic elements and especially of the planets on man and his activities. The Four White Horses Hall thus leads to the subject-matter of the ceiling paintings of the Stone Rooms, which are dedicated to nature and the cosmos.

Paintings on the walls

The walls of the Four White Horses Hall were originally covered predominantly with architectural perspectives in scagliola. Today they are hung with five paintings of the Dutchman Paolo Fiammingo (active in Venice) which adequately supplement the planet programme of the ceiling. Made from about 1592, they show starting from the left in clockwise direction Apollo (science and the arts), Venus (dance), Mars (war), Mercury (commerce) and Diana (agriculture).

The paintings were originally possibly intended for the Fugger Palace at Kirchheim a.d. Mindel; in 1770 they were located in Schleissheim Palace.

The doors of the Four White Horses Hall like those of the Imperial Hall are modeled on the door between the Four White Horses Hall and the Stone Rooms, which is the only preserved original door. Chairs and chandeliers of both halls are modern productions.

111 Imperial Hall   *Fig. 14*

The "Imperial Hall" so-called only from 1673, measures around 34 x 15 m, with a height of around 10 m extending through the main floor and the mezzanine. It originally possessed on both sides five high rectangular double windows with round windows above and - in the mezzanine area - small rectangular windows; the original arrangement has been kept today only in the south side facing the Imperial Courtyard. In the course of the remodelling under Max IV Joseph, the window axes on the North side facing the Court Garden were changed; in the current reconstruction, the windows of the north side were closed - in a manner invisible from the outside - to obtain surfaces for hanging tapestries. On the two narrow sides, large upright structures of stucco made to simulate marble: On the original entrance side adjoining the Imperial Stairs a majestic portal, and a stately fireplace (fireplace framing is of Adnet marble) on the side next to the Four White Horses Hall, which once also formed the main face. At the side, they are flanked by two considerably smaller passages with framings from stucco made to resemble marble. For structural reasons, the coffered ceiling of the hall is made of stucco, and not as originally of wood.

Ceiling paintings

Completed in 1614/15 by Peter Candid and his studio. The three central ceiling paintings, are colour-matched, full-scale photographic reproductions of the originals which were burnt in 1944.

The central octagonal ceiling picture: Allegory of Earthly Fame (as the accompanying texts elucidate, Magnanimity scorns Honour and Praise, which are pursued by Ambition). At the side: Two paintings with Roman and Egyptian architectural objects (antique memorials).

Octagonal ceiling painting of the side to the Four White Horses Hall: Allegory of World Supremacy (below represented by Nebuchadnezzar or Nimrod, Cyrus or Darius, Alexander and Caesar or Augustus - the four worldly realms of antiquity: Assyria, Persia, Greece, Rome; above enthroned on clouds at left Sovereign Power, at right Foresighted Wisdom, in between and hovering Victorious Virtue). Putti with weapons and war trophies on the eight surrounding paintings.

Octagonal ceiling painting on the side toward the Imperial Stairs: Allegory of Wisdom (the enthroned figure of Wisdom is surrounded by the Seven Liberal

Arts and the Sciences). Putti with the attributes of the Seven Liberal Arts and the Sciences on the eight surrounding pictures.

As a whole the ceiling programme indicates that the sovereign ruling wisely and guided by virtue, who does not strive for fleeting fame, must exercise his office equally in war and peace, in both the military and civil sphere.

Frieze pictures

On the Court Garden side and the Imperial Courtyard side eight representations each of exemplary deeds from Biblical-Judaic and pagan-antique history, probably Andrea Vicentino, Venice shortly before 1613.

The scenes from the Old Testament and the history of antiquity facing each other are related to each other both with regard to content and composition and usually are placed under a common virtue. In addition, a male figure alternates each time with a female figure. Painting pairs (from west to east): Esther before Ahasuerus as well as Veturia before Coriolanus (female selflessness in the petition); Jael and Sisara as well as Penthesilea and Achilles (female daring); Samson and Delilah as well as Hercules and Antaeus (defeat of the strong heroes by love); Judith with the head of Holofernes as well as Tomyris with the head of Cyrus (victory by a woman over the man weakened through intemperance); David and Goliath as well as Marcus Valerius Corvinus (victory of the weaker over stronger through trust in God); Susanna and the Elders as well as Tarquin and Lucretia (chastity); Judas Maccabaeus as well as Horatius Cocles (bravery); Moses and Lycurgus (wisdom in legislation).

Tapestries

Five tapestries with Old Testament heroes and heroines (Gideon, Deborah, Eleazar, Michal, Joseph) completed after the cartoons by Peter Candid by the weavers Hans van der Biest and Hans van den Bosschen in Enghien, 1615-1618.

Signature and weaver mark of Hans van der Biest and city mark of Enghien. In contrast to the other tapestries of the Munich Residence after Peter Candid's designs, wool is predominantly used for the less finely woven tapestries, and only a little silk and no gold material. The picture panels represent the heroes and heroines as monumental single figures in usually fanciful apparel and armour; the action in the small-scale-background is depicted in greater detail.

Five of the eleven (originally twelve) Imperial Hall tapestries now hang on the north side. In each case, a tapestry with a female figure is associated with a frieze painting containing a male figure as the primary subject, and vice versa; for example, there is found - under the concept of chastity - the Old Testament Joseph beneath the Old Testament Susanna. In all, various virtues appositely exemplified by characters from both the Bible and Classical antiquity - with an equal number of males and females - are shown in the frieze paintings and the tapestries.

Bronze sculpture (on the fireplace)
"Tellus Bavarica", Hubert Gerhard, Munich about 1590.

Originally there was a porphyry statue of Virtus (Virtue), on the mantelpiece, which provides the key to the iconographic programme of the Imperial Hall. This was lost and, since 1985, the bronze Tellus Bavarica, the personification of Bavaria, created by Hubert Gerhard around 1590 was displayed there in 1985. A salt-barrel and water urn lie at her feet, alluding to Bavaria's abundance of salt and water; in addition, the helmeted figure formerly bore in her right hand a garland of wheat ears as reference to rich grain harvests. Deerhide and hunting-horn stand for the profusion of game in the country and the successful hunt. The sculpture, originally conceived as fountain figure, was transferred after 1616 to the newly erected Tempietto in the large Court Garden (a bronze copy is now there).

112 Imperial Staircase   *Fig. 13*

The stairway with festive and leisurely ascent is formed by three straight flights - in a dog-leg arrangement -, which opens towards the upper landing with wide arches; the shorter third flight leads to the mezzanine floor. The transverse arches rest on paired Tuscan columns (formerly of marble, but today of stucco simulating marble) and on double pilasters (of stucco simulating marble). Probably the first monumental stair layout in Germany, it was inspired by exemplars found principally in Genoese palaces.

The figural motifs in the painted grotesque decoration of the stair vault refer in some cases to the subject-matter of the Imperial Hall: In the lower flight the apotheosis of the virtuous hero Hercules, correspondingly in the middle flight of stairs, small-figural scenes with the deeds of Hercules; and in the upper

183

flight, the fall of Icarus as symbol of human presumptuousness. Further scenes of hunting and rural occupations. - The vault paintings were executed up to 1616 by Hans Donauer the Younger, Hans Oberhofer, Hans Stroia and Johann Baptist Geyrer; the stuccowork was done by Matthias Piechl and Kaspar Marolt. Reconstruction by Karl Manninger from the 1967 to 1975 using photographs.

Niche figures

On the walls of the stairwell shaft: On the lower landing at the right, Palatine Count Otto von Wittelsbach, the first Bavarian duke (since 1180) from the Wittelsbach Dynasty. - On the lower landing at the left: Emperor Charlemagne, according to former historical theory, ancestor of the Wittelsbachs; surmounted by a relief showing an allegory of the church. - On the middle flight of stairs: Emperor Ludwig the Bavarian, first emperor of the Wittelsbach Dynasty; as crowning relief depiction of Victory. All three stucco figures about 1616 by Hans Krumper.

Busts

Above the side entrances to the Imperial Hall, the busts of two Wittelsbachs, who were called as rulers to foreign thrones: At the left Otto III of Lower Bavaria, King of Hungary 1305-1312; at the right Albert III of Upper Bavaria-Munich and Straubing, who in 1440 declined the Bohemian royal crown which had been offered to him. Above the large central entrance, the inscription of the builder Maximilian I.

In the overall sceme with the Imperial Hall, the virtues of the rulers in the programme of the Imperial Stairs are not expressed in terms of the Old Testament and antique history, but rather in the history of Bavaria and especially that of the Wittelsbach dynasty: The ancestors of Maximilian I themselves become heroes of virtue.

184

From the Imperial Stairs, Room 112, back through Rooms 111-108 to the Room of the Seasons, Room 107. From here, go through the door in the fireplace wall into the Connecting Room, Room 113.

113 Connecting Room

Sculpture

Bronze statue of Otto von Wittelsbach, the first Bavarian duke from the Wittelsbach Dynasty (since 1180), by Hubert Gerhard, Munich 1592/93, cast, by Martin Frey, Munich in 1593.

Originally intended - under the name of Theodo (the legendary first Christian Duke von Bavaria) - for the tomb of Wilhelm V; since about 1610 centrally placed on the Wittelsbach Fountain described on pages 23-24 (replaced there today by a bronze copy), and traditionally interpreted as Otto von Wittelsbach.

114 Theatiner Corridor

The long gallery-room with 16 window apertures was built beween 1613 and 1616 (completion date on the southern portal framing). The stuccowork, rolled forms with acanthus tendrils, cartouches and reliefs (putti with emblems) by Michael Castelli after designs by Hans Krumper. Portal framings in red stucco simulating marble. Badly damaged in World War II the stuccowork and door frames have been heavily restored. The original painted decoration is lost.

At the north end of the corridor, on the left, a portal closed before 1700, which formerly led to the battlements of the city wall and from around 1670 was linked to the Theatine Monastery.

Opposite a wrought iron grille from the construction period which provides a view into the Hans-Steininger Stairway with original stuccowork and remains of paintings after designs by Hans Krumper (1615/16).

The portals of the inside wall lead into the spandrel rooms between the Theatiner Corridor and Stone Rooms.

CIRCULAR TOUR II LEADS BACK TO THE GOLDEN HALL (ROOM 71) AND CONTINUES IN THE "KÖNIGS-BAU" (ROYAL PALACE) IN THE APARTMENTS OF THE QUEEN AND OF THE KING (ROOMS 72, 115-127).

72, 115-127 The "Königsbau" (Royal Palace)

When Max IV Joseph became the first Bavarian king in 1806, he had no royal residence appropriate to his new rank. However, the devastating ravages of war meant that the Bavarian finances were completely exhausted. The king considered himself as a "Citizen King" and therefore had no intention to build a special royal residence for himself. His son Ludwig, on the other hand, understood even as Crown Prince the royal function awaiting him and primarily considered this as a royal dignity. Consequently, even before his reign began, he commissioned Leo von Klenze in 1824 to draw up plans for a royal residence. This was the "Königsbau", a component of the magnificent building ensemble of the Max-Joseph-Platz. The king's reverence for Italy and the Renaissance determined the architectural style, particularly that of the main façade, which - in imitation of the architecture of the early Florentine Renaissance - was composed of elements taken from the Palazzo Pitti and the Palazzo Rucellai. The corner-stone was laid on 18th June 1826, the anniversary of Napoleon's defeat at Waterloo. The "Königsbau" (Royal Palace) was completed in 1835; it was occupied in the same year on the date of the Silver Wedding Anniversary of the royal couple.

The ground floor contains festive halls, the "Nibelungen Halls" (Rooms 75-79), and formerly was to accommodate a library as well. The royal apartments were located on the main floor.

Their sequence corresponded largely to the canon of the 17th and 18th century, as had been used earlier in the Residence, namely: Several antechambers, audience chamber or throne room, bedroom and private cabinet or study or small library. Whereas during the Age of Absolutism, the apartments of the prince and his wife were still separate from each other, they now join in the middle of the building so that the reception rooms are located at the extreme ends and the more private rooms meet in the middle. This is an innovation, which was first introduced in the etiquette of the Napoleonic Era. However a prototype for this is already to be found in the apartments of the Elector Max III Joseph (the so-called Electoral Chambers, Rooms 22-31) in the Munich Residence. It is also an innovation for Munich that the royal chambers are accessible by means of two large stairways at the ends of the building, in other words the so-called "Yellow Staircase" for the King and the "Queen-Mother-Staircase" for the Queen, in addition to the large shaft staircase in the centre of the building. This however, served only the private chambers located in the northern part of the building. Also new is that the royal chambers lie within the public view so to speak; this was also an intention of the king, who prided himself on getting up early: "My light is always the first one when I look out on the Max-Joseph-Platz in the morning, only gradually do the lights go on in the bourgeois houses."

The king also specified the pictorial programme of the paintings of his chambers: The royal suite is completely dedicated to the classical that is Greek poetry. The queen's chambers contain picture programs from the zenith of German poetry from Walther von der Vogelweide up to Klopstock and Bürger, Wieland, Goethe and Schiller.

Leo von Klenze also designed the furniture specifically for the individual rooms of the two apartments, and this was made exclusively by Munich cabinet-makers (among which Melchior Frank, Leonhard Glink, Johann Baptist Hemmer and Joseph Pössenbacher) and sculptors (Johann Ernst Mayer and others) in 1834/35. The Parisian dealer Larnaz Tribout supplied most of the gilt bronzes. However, also bronze-foundries and girdlers in Munich and Nuremberg produced various items in gilt bronze, which were made after designs by Leo von Klenze.

Although these rooms were heavily damaged in 1944, thanks to a descriptive room-inventory of 1835, it was possible, by 1980, to refurbish and reappoint them as they had been in 1835 when the Royal Palace was completed. This was most fortunate, since subsequent generations of rulers had drastically altered the furnishings. Starting in 1849, King Max II had partly refurnished the rooms, so that the severe, indeed plain, character of the chambers as conceived by Ludwig gave way for living comfort and convenience. This was in striking contrast to the programme of his father, who had expressly forbidden panellings, silk hangings and wall mirrors. Consequently, after 1849, Ludwig I refused to enter the Royal Palace ever again.

With the completion of the Royal Apartments in 1980, a suite from the time of King Ludwig I has been resurrected which is quite unique after the destruction of Munich. An unrivalled ensemble of painting, sculpture, furniture and textile appointments has newly arisen in the Royal Palace. And so, the Royal Palace today once again represents the endeavour of King Ludwig I to make Munich a city of the arts and muses.

The "Königsbau" (Royal Palace) was restored using the evidence of preserved fragments of the wall decoration, that is the frescoes and the encaustic paintings and stuccowork, and also of photographs (including colour-photographs) which record its appearence before the destruction. In particular, the inlaid floors were restored, but the once very elaborate ornamentation had to be somewhat reduced. The rooms located to the north could not be restored. Also the former antechambers of the king, now accessible as the "Battle Halls" (Rooms 14a-14c), suffered such severe and extensive damage that it was impossible to reconstruct their original décor. On the other hand it was possible to partially restore the adjoining suite.

The reconstruction of the decoration of the walls, ceilings and floors is almost completely true to the original. Moreover, virtually all the furniture was preserved, as well as the chandeliers, candelabra and clocks. The textiles and soft furnishings, i.e. the furniture coverings, the window draperies and the canopies were restored from preserved parts and rediscovered fragments.

The floors are inlaid with precious woods. Technique of the wall painting: Encaustic, the ceiling paintings in stucco framings: Fresco. Furniture in spruce, painted white and gilded (in the elegant Rooms 118, 119, 126 and 127 completely gilded); only the furniture of the more simply furnished antechambers Rooms 115/116 is veneered in walnut.

The Queen's Apartment

115 First Antechamber

Only the inlaid wooden floor could be restored on the evidence of old photographs; the former elaborate wall decoration with the pictures from the life and the poems of Walther von der Vogelweide by Gottlieb Gassen is lost.

Furnishings

A two-door wardrobe as well as three chests, walnut with light boxwood marquetry, all painted with the coat of arms of the Kingdom of Bavaria, the latter originally used as bed chests for the servants. - Six chairs with (restored) green leather coverings, walnut with light maple marquetry. - A secretary with monogram "T" (Queen Therese), an armchair, a stool and a footstool; palisander with light maple marquetry.

116 Second Antechamber

Here likewise, it was possible to restore the intarsia floor by reference to photographs, but not the paintings by Carl Heinrich Hermann after Wolfram von Eschenbach's "Parsifal" which once decorated the walls and the ceiling.

Furniture

Two wardrobes as in the First Antechamber, with painted royal coat of arms.

117 Service Room

Most of the paintings by Philipp Foltz (in association with Theodor Dietz and Alois Wendling) of scenes from the poems of Gottlieb August Bürger survived or could be restored.

Entrance wall: "The Wild Huntsman" - "Lenore" (destroyed).

Exit wall: Below: "Song of the Good Man" - "The Grey Friar and the Female Pilgrim" - above: "The Abduction" (Ravishing of Gertrud) - "Bürger at Home" - "Song of Faithfulness" (The Faithful Dogs).

Window side (facing Max-Joseph-Platz): Two scenes from "Leonardo and Blandine".

Window side (facing Residenzstrasse): Below: "Unfaithfulness over Everything" (Bürger with Molly Leonhart) - "The Loyal Wives of Weinsberg" - Above: "The Abduction" (The Reconciliation).

The stove in the niche on the east side has been destroyed.

Furnishings

Four fauteuils and six chairs with blue silk coverings, painted in white and gold, with facing sphinxes on the backrest (see also Room 14a). The desk formerly located here is now in the

Queen's writing cabinet (Room 121). Curtains of blue silk (like the furniture coverings).

Twelve-branched chandelier with 24 lamps, Franz Sales Sauter, Munich about 1833/35.
After a design by Leo von Klenze. Gilt bronze.

118 Throne Room   *Fig. 36*

With the exception of most of the pictorial scenes, the decoration could be reconstructed. The pictures in the frieze and in the ceiling were by Wilhelm Kaulbach and showed scenes from the poems of Friedrich Gottlieb Klopstock.

Even for interior decoration of the 19th century, the wall decoration is surprising and unique: above a lapis-lazuli blue stucco baseboard, the wall is completely gilded and covered with a palmette network ornamentation. Between the palmettes, continuous rows of lozenges with alternating monograms of Ludwig and Therese.

Furnishings

Seating furniture coverings, canopy and curtains are of purple-red silk velvet (that of the canopy and the curtains renewed).

Two elaborately carved console tables with marble tops on griffins supported by small genii. - The throne and two fauteuils with armrests supported by sphinxes are completely gilded as are the eight chairs. The monogram of Queen Marie (wife of King Maximilian II) in the throne was added later.

The chandelier of gilt bronze has eight branches ending in griffin bodies, delivered by Larnaz Tribout, Paris c. 1833/35. - Four gilt bronze candelabra each on three columns, with griffins, which carry the candlestick; after the model of the candelabra by Larnaz Tribout, located in Room 119, by Franz Sales Sauter, Munich c. 1833/35.

Two clocks, delivered by Larnaz Tribout, Paris c. 1833/35.
Gilt bronze. Warrior with helmet as well as the Theban field marshal Epaminondas, who (mortally wounded in the battle of Mantineia) pulls the spear from his breast.

119 Salon

The painted wall decoration in Pompeiian style is largely restored. The wall pictures after a design by Wilhelm Kaulbach (painted by Ernst Förster) show scenes from the poems of Christoph Martin Wieland, as does the (reconstructed) frieze by Eugen Napoleon Neureuther. While the wall paintings show scenes from "Musarion" and the "Graces", the pictures in the frieze are devoted to scenes from "Oberon".

Furnishings
The stove is no longer preserved.
The furniture coverings as well as the curtains are of carmine red damask with fine floral decoration.
The lounge with armrests in the shape of swans, the six fauteuils and the twenty chairs as well as the round table and the console table with griffin ends are completely gilded.

Two candelabra in gilt bronze, delivered by Larnaz Tribout, Paris c. 1833-1835, after a design by Leo von Klenze, (model for the candelabra in Room 118 copied by Franz Sales Sauter). - Chandelier in gilt bronze with twelve branches and 54 lamps, delivered by Larnaz Tribout, Paris c. 1833-1835.

Clock, Joseph Biergans, Munich about 1842.
Gilt Bronze. The clock, with seated figures of Ceres was originally created for the small games room in the Banquet Hall building.

120 Bedroom

The appearence of the room was largely regained through the reconstruction; remnants of the murals painted by Wilhelm Kaulbach with the assistance of Ernst Förster, Daniel Engelmann and Robert Lecke were preserved. They show scenes from Goethe's Works (on the entrance wall three scenes from "Faust", on the rear wall, two scenes from "Iphigenie", on the exit wall three scenes from "Egmont"). In compliance with an express order of the king that no wall hangings or tapestries should be used in the "Königsbau" (Royal Palace), the walls were painted to simulate green wall hanings.

Furnishings

The furniture painted in white and gold is covered with green damask from which the curtains are also made.

Two bedside tables, called somnos, with depictions of owls belong to the two beds which are decorated with genii. - A low lounge is in the middle of the room. - The backrests of the two fauteuils as well as those of the eight chairs are supported by dolphins (Klenze's authorship is uncertain).

Two candelabra in part gilt bronze, probably German about 1835 (from the rear parlor of the queen). - Chandelier of gilt bronze with a total of 36 lamp branches on two levels, crowned by a column with flame bowl, produced by the bronze factory of Carl von Moy in Munich about 1833-1835, probably to a design by Leo von Klenze.

Clock, delivered by Larnaz Tribout, Paris about 1833-1835.
Gilt bronze. The clock shows the Infant Bacchus on a chariot, drawn by a panisc and accompanied by a putto.

121 Writing Cabinet *Fig. 37*

Above a baseboard finished in Pompeiian red, perpendicular rectangular panels in green with scenes from Schiller's poems by Wilhelm Lindenschmit and Philipp Foltz. The grotesque decorations on the barrel vault were painted by Gaiani and Georg Schilling. Whereas the narratives on the vault were destroyed, those on the walls have largely survived.

Entrance wall: Three scenes from "The Way to the Blacksmith".

Rear wall: "The Glove", "The Count of Habsburg", "The Diver".

Exit wall: Three scenes from "Knight Toggenburg".

Window wall: "German Faithfulness" (Reconciliation between Emperor Ludwig the Bavarian and Friedrich the Handsome of Austria) - "Graf Eberhard der Greiner".

Furnishings

Curtains and furniture coverings of green damask.

The furniture is painted white and gilded. To the original décor belong: Two armchairs and four chairs (Klenze's authorship is uncertain), the round and the rectangular table, the writing chair, the six-sided wastepaper basket, the letter- or writing box and the folding table as well as the vanity table and the four side tables with lyre frame. - The desk comes from the Queen's Service Hall (Room 117) and bears the monogram of Queen Therese; its top is borne by four lion monopodes. - Two corner sofas.

Bowl-shaped chandelier with six arms and 18 lights, of gilt bronze, made by the girdler Christian Block, Munich c. 1833-1835.

Writing utensils, Paris or Munich c. 1830-1835.

Gilt Bronze. Two amorettes flank an oval medallion, which used to contain the monogram of Ludwig I.

122 Library Room

Of the paintings by Moritz von Schwind with scenes from the poems of Ludwig Tieck, only the lunette opposite the window wall with a scene from "Prince Zerbino" is extant: The muse of poetry surrounded by Dante, Tasso, Ariosto, Cervantes and Shakespeare as well as Goethe, Schiller, Wieland, Herder and Klopstock. On the ceiling several paintings copied from colour photographs.

Furnishings

The library cabinets in white and gold were reconstructed. - The white glazed stove on the rear wall is lost. Belonging to the original furnishings are the library table on twelve column-legs as well as the two chairs and the armchair with blue damask ("Gourgouran"). The curtains are also of the same material.

The chandelier of gilt bronze comes from the Court Garden Rooms and was made early in the 19th century.

The King's Apartment

123 Bedroom

The decorative part of the wall paintings in Pompeiian style has been reconstructed, while the pictorial scenes (from the poems of Theocritus) were destroyed apart from a few fragments. They were painted from designs by Heinrich Maria Heß by Leopold Schulz, Alexander Bruckmann and Wilhelm Röckel. On the entrance wall a scene from the "Small Heracles" (Teiresias prophesies to the mother Alkmene, the mother of Heracles, hero's fate awaiting her son) as well as the picture of Eros riding on a wild boar have been preserved.

The white stucco reliefs on blue ground after Berthel Thorwaldsen's model (Rome 1818) represent "Night" and "Morning".

Furnishings

Furniture in white and gold: Two commodes, two armchairs, four chairs, a bed with genii in the carriage team, a bedside table ("Somno") as well as a round table on three lion monopodes. The coverings and the curtains are of green damask ("Cannetillé").

Four bronze candelabra, patinated green and gilded, probably Munich, second quarter of the 19th century.

124 Dressing room

The pictures in the coffered barrel vault and on the walls after designs by Ludwig Michael Schwanthaler (painted by Johann Georg Hiltensperger) with scenes from the comedies of Aristophanes were almost completely destroyed; the sole-survivors are on the window side, at the top right: The Birds conclude Peace with Hercules, Poseidon and Triballos (from "The Birds") and below: The Dog Trial (from "The Wasps").

Furnishings

Furniture coverings and curtains are of red damask. - Furniture painted in white and gold: A large table, lounge with footstool, wastepaper basket, small round table, walking stick stand, four armchairs.

Two gilt bronze candelabra by Larnaz Tribout, Paris 1833-1835 (from the Queen's Service Hall, Room 117). - Lavabo of gilt bronze with ewer and basin, by the girdler Franz Sales Sauter and the goldsmith Joseph Weber, after a design by Leo von Klenze, Munich 1835.

125 Study

The bookcases originally stood against the grey-green walls. Notable is the gorgeous white marble fireplace with figural and ornamental decoration.

All the paintings were destroyed; they formerly showed scenes from the tragedies of Sophocles after designs by Ludwig Michael Schwanthaler.

Furnishings

Furniture painted in white and gold: Two commodes; four console tables on volutes ending in lion's paws, with mirrored rear wall (not belonging to the original furnishing of the room); two chairs, covered with green silk, which was also used for the curtains.

The 12 gilt bronze statuettes of Wittelsbach princes are reductions made about 1840 from the large gilt bronze figures after designs by Ludwig Michael Schwanthaler, which originally stood in the Throne Room of the Banquet Hall Building and today are displayed in the Staircase Hall of the New Hercules Hall:

Otto II the Illustrious, Duke of Bavaria, 1206-1253; Ludwig IV the Bavarian, Duke of Bavaria, Emperor, 1282-1347; Rupprecht III, Elector of the Palatinate, German King, 1352-1410; Friedrich I the Victorious, Elector of the Palatinate, 1425-1476; Ludwig IX the Rich, Duke of Bavaria-Landshut, 1417-1479; Albrecht IV, Duke of Bavaria, 1447-1508; Friedrich II the Wise, Elector of the Palatinate, 1482-1556; Albrecht V, Duke of Bavaria, 1528-1579; Maximilian I, Elector of Bavaria, 1573-1651; Karl XI, Duke of Zweibrücken-Kleeburg, King of Sweden, 1655-1697; Johann Wilhelm, Elector of the Palatinate, 1658-1716; Karl XII, Duke of Zweibrücken-Kleeburg, King of Sweden, 1682-1718.

Three clocks in gilt bronze, designed by Ludwig Michael Schwanthaler for the Banquet Hall Building.

On the mantelpiece: Clock with the equestrian figure of Emperor Ludwig the Bavarian, made by Rudolf Jakoby, Vienna 1842.

At the side: Two clocks with King Rudolf of Habsburg (1218-1291), at the left with cross and imperial orb, at the right crowned by the Pope, Paris about 1842, the works of the left clock signed by Japy Frères (probably Fritz, Louis and Pierre Japy; from the Hall of Rudolf of Habsburg).

Four candelabra each with eight branches and a central lamp, gilt bronze, perhaps Munich about 1842, probably after a design by Leo von Klenze (from the Banquet Hall Building).

126 Reception Room

Because of the almost completely reconstructed Pompeiian wall decoration, this intimate room is one of the loveliest in the suite of the royal chambers. The pictures on the walls and on the vault - with scenes from the tragedies of Aeschylus - after designs by Ludwig Michael Schwanthaler (painted by Philipp Anton Schilgen) were destroyed.

Furnishings

The round table with marble top and the six chairs are completely gilded; chair coverings of (renewed) blue-green morocco leather with gold impression. The curtains are made of royal blue damask.

Four floor candelabra of gilt bronze for six candles, cast in the foundry of Johann Baptist Stiglmaier, Munich about 1833-1835.
Candelabra arms by Franz Xaver Eisendorf. After a design by Leo von Klenze.

Busts

Caesar and Frederick the Great, , probably Munich c. 1833-1835.
Cast bronze (Frederick the Great) and chased copper (Caesar). The bases of yellow marble after a design by Leo von Klenze.

127 Throne Room   *Fig. 38*

Reliefs and wall structure are white against a golden background; the undisturbed dual harmony lends the room increased solemnity. Only the canopy and the throne both covered with purple-red silk velvet and the curtains from the same material stand out in colour.

The pictorial programme of the hall, taken from Pindar's odes, was completely reconstructed.

On the entrance wall starting from the left-hand door: "Dioscuri" and "Graces" - "Life in the Elysian Fields" (tympanum) - "Deucalion and Pyrrha" (below the tympanum) - "The Horae" and "Erection of an Apollo temple in Rhodes" (above the right-hand door).

Rear wall: "Bellerophon tames Pegasus" and "Founding of the Olympic Games by Heracles" (above the left-hand door). - "Heracles" - "Heracles strangles the Snakes" - "Heracle's Struggle with Antaeus" (at the left of the throne, from bottom to top) - "Achilles" - "Peleus and Thetis" - "Achilles and Patroclus" (at the right of the throne, from bottom to top) - "Building of Thebes" and "Death of Medusa" (above the right-hand door).

Exit wall: "Death of Ajas" and "Clytaemnestra's Death" (above the left-hand door) - "Typhoeus and the Muses" (tympanum above) - "Hera and the Three Fates" (below the tympanum) - "Apollo with Chiron" and "Death of Neoptolemos" (above the right-hand door).

Window wall: "Castor and Pollux as Horse-Tamers" - "Castor's Death through Idas and Lynceus" - "Castor and Polydeuces" (at the left from the middle, from top to bottom) - "Jason and Medea" - "Jason with only one Shoe" - "Jason and the Fiery Bulls" (at the right from the middle, from bottom to top).

Frieze: Rear wall: "Pindar recites his Odes to the People" (in the middle over the throne). - Over the doors: "Contest of Poetry" (at the left) - "Competition in Music" (at the right) - in between "Olympia" and "Pythia" as symbols of the Games. - On the other walls depictions of the Olympian, Pythian and Nemean Contests (Chariot Racing, Wrestling, Boxing, Running, Horse-Racing, Award of Prizes).

Furnishings

The throne with embroidered monogram of Ludwig I made in 1842 in Munich originally stood in the Throne Room of the Banquet Hall Building. The canopy dome has been reconstructed as has the velvet drapery; the Bavarian royal coat of

arms in gold and silver embroidery on the rear wall is original.
- Two gilded console tables on lion monopodes with white marble tops, Munich about 1834/35.

Four candelabra with seven branches and a central lamp, made of gilt bronze, delivered by Larnaz Tribout, Paris c. 1833-1835.
- Two large chandeliers with four lamp-wreaths arranged above each other, of gilt bronze, delivered by Larnaz Tribout, Paris c. 1833-1835, after a design by Leo von Klenze.

Two clocks, delivered by Larnaz Tribout, Paris c. 1833-1835.
On the left a depiction of Urania, at the right depiction of the Blind Belizar.

THE ROYAL APARTMENTS OF THE "KÖNIGSBAU" ARE AGAIN TRAVERSED IN REVERSE ORDER UNTIL THE QUEEN-MOTHER-STAIRCASE (ROOM 72, page 130) IS REACHED. THIS IS TAKEN TO REACH THE GROUND-FLOOR ROOMS OF THE "KÖNIGSBAU" (ROYAL PALACE) - THE NIBELUNGEN HALLS (ROOMS 73-81, page 131-133), WHICH CONSTITUTE THE CONCLUSION OF CIRCULAR TOUR I.

BIBLIOGRAPHY

Christian Haeutle (Hrsg.): Die Reisen des Augsburgers Philipp Hainhofer nach Eichstätt, München und Regensburg in den Jahren 1611, 1612 und 1613. In: Zeitschrift des Historischen Vereins für Schwaben und Neuburg 8, 1881, S. 1-316

Baldassar Pistorini: Descrittione compendiosa del palagio sede de' Serenissimi di Baviera. Situato nella elettorale città di Monaco (Handschrift von 1644 in der Bayer. Staatsbibliothek, Cod. Ital. 409, S. 71 ff.)

Ranuccio Pallavicino: I trionfi dell' Architettura nella sontuosa Residenza di Monaco descritti e rappresentati all' Altezza Serren. di Ferdinando Maria Duca dell' una e l'altra Baviera.... München 1667, Nachdruck Augsburg 1680

Johann Schmidt: Triumphierendes Wunder-Gebaew Der Chur-Fuerstlichen Residenz zu München. München 1685

Michael Wening: Historico-Topographica Descriptio... Band 1, Rentamt München. München 1701 (Residenzbeschreibung S. 3-8).

Christoph Kalmbach: Triumphierendes Wunder-Gebäu Der Chur-Fürstlichen Residenz zu München. München 1719

Lorenz von Westenrieder: Beschreibung der Haupt- und Residenzstadt München. München 1782 (Residenzbeschreibung S. 51 ff.)

Johann Sebastian von Rittershausen: Die vornehmste Merkwürdigkeiten der Residenzstadt München für Liebhaber der bildenden Künste. München 1787, Nachdruck München 1788 (Residenzbeschreibung S. 3 ff.)

Ernst Förster: Leitfaden zur Betrachtung der Wand- und Deckenbilder des neuen Königsbaues in München. München 1834

Johann Michael Söltl: München mit seinen Umgebungen, historisch, topographisch, statistisch dargestellt. München 1838 (Residenzbeschreibung S. 176 ff.)

Felix Schiller: München, dessen Kunstschätze, Umgebungen und öffentliches Leben. München 1841 (Residenzbeschreibung S. 64 ff.)

(Leo von Klenze:) Die Dekoration der inneren Räume des Königsbaues zu München... Sonderdruck aus: Allgemeine Bauzeitung, Wien 1842

Rudolf und Hermann Marggraff: München mit seinen Kunstschätzen und Merkwürdigkeiten nebst Ausflügen in die Umgegend, vornehmlich nach Hohenschwangau und Augsburg, München 1846 (Residenzbeschreibung S. 273 ff.)

Le Palais du roi à Munich, München 1852

Joseph von Hefner: Die Grottenhalle und das Grottenhöfchen in der königlichen alten Residenz zu München. In: Oberbayerisches Archiv 21, H. 2, 1859, S. 153-166

Franz Reber: Bautechnischer Führer durch München 1876 (Residenzbeschreibung S. 243 ff.)

Leonhard Enzler, Jacob Stockbauer und Franz Xaver Zettler: Ausgewählte Kunstwerke aus dem Schatze der Reichen Capelle in der Königlichen Residenz zu München. München 1876

Georg Friedrich Seidel: Die Königliche Residenz in München (32 Kupferstiche und 3 Farbendrucke). Leipzig 1880

Christian Haeutle: Geschichte der Residenz in München von ihren frühesten Zeiten bis herab zum Jahre 1777. Leipzig 1883

Otto Aufleger: Die Reichen Zimmer der Königl. Residenz in München, mit geschichtl. Einl. von Karl Trautman. München 1893

Georg Böttger: Die Innenräume der königl. Alten Residenz in München. München 1893-1895

Otto Aufleger und Wolfgang Maria Schmid: Führer durch die k. Residenz zu München. München 1897, [2]1908

Die Kunstdenkmale des Regierungsbezirkes Oberbayern. Teil 2: Stadt München (von Gustav von Bezold, Berthold Riehl und Georg Hager). München 1902 (Residenzbeschreibung S. 1070 ff.)

Führer durch die Kgl. Residenz München mit Anhang der Sehenswürdigkeiten der Stadt München. München 1908

Friedrich H. Hofmann: Frankenthaler Porzellan. 2 Bde. München 1911

Friedrich H. Hofmann: Die Residenz als Museum. In: Bayerland 31, Nr. 19, 1920, S. 303-318

Friedrich H. Hofmann: Geschichte der Bayerischen Porzellan-Manufaktur Nymphenburg. 3 Bde. Leipzig 1921-1923

Hans Buchheit und Rudolf Oldenburg: Das Miniaturenkabinett der Münchner Residenz. München 1921

Armin Hausladen: Köstlichkeiten aus dem Münchener Residenzmuseum. München 1922

Adolf Feulner: Das Residenzmuseum in München. München 1922

Max Frankenburger: Die Silberkammer der Münchner Residenz. München 1923

Heinrich Goebel: Wandteppiche. 6 Bde. Leipzig 1923-1934

Adolf Feulner: Katalog der Gemälde im Residenzmuseum München und in Schloß Nymphenburg. München 1924

Adolf Feulner: Münchens Fürstenschlösser. Stuttgart o. J. (1930)

Hans Thoma und Heinrich Kreisel: Residenz München. Amtl. Führer. München 1937

Hans Thoma: Die Münchener Residenz. Bremen 1938

Fritz Haeberlein: Schatzkammer der Reichen Kapelle. München 1939

Luisa Hager: Ein Majolika-Tafelgeschirr aus Faenza im Residenzmuseum München. In: Pantheon 23, 1939, S. 135-139

Luisa Hager: Die Majolika-Kredenz Herzog Wilhelms V. in der Residenz München. In: Pantheon 30, 1942, S. 228-231

Festschrift zur Eröffnung des Fest- und Konzertsaales in der Münchener Residenz am 3. März 1953. München 1953

Hans R. Weihrauch: Die Bildwerke in Bronze und anderen Metallen (Bayerisches Nationalmuseum, Katalog XIII, 5). München 1956, Anhang S. 210 ff.

Erwin Schalkhaußer: Die Münchener Schule in der Stuckdekoration des 17. Jahrhunderts. In: Oberbayerisches Archiv 81/82, 1957, S. 1-139

Erwin Schalkhaußer: Die Hofkapelle der Münchener Residenz. In: Das Münster 11, 1958, S. 261-266

Festschrift zur Eröffnung des Alten Residenztheaters in München (Cuvilliés-Theater). München 1958

Festschrift zur Wiedereröffnung des Residenzmuseums München. München 1958

Hans Thoma und Herbert Brunner: Schatzkammer der Residenz München. München 1958 (Neuauflagen 1969 und 1970)

Herbert Brunner: Altes Residenztheater in München (Cuvilliés-Theater). Amtl. Führer. München 1958 (letzte Neuauflage 1990)

Erich Hubala: Ein Entwurf für das Antiquarium der Münchner Residenz 1568. In: Münchner Jahrbuch der bildenden Kunst 3. F. 9/10, 1958/1959, S. 128-146

Kurt Hentzen: Der Hofgarten zu München. München 1959

Vierte Festschrift zum Wiederaufbau der Residenz München. Ausbau des Festsaalflügels an der Nordostecke der Residenz für die Bayerische Akademie der Wis-senschaften. München 1959

Sepp Huf: Wiederaufbau der Münchner Residenz. In: Deutsche Kunst- und Denkmalpflege 17, 1959, S. 1-16

Residenz München. Sonderausgabe der Zeitschrift Bayerland 62, Nr. 4, 1960

Herbert Brunner: Altes Tafelsilber. München 1964

Oswald Hederer: Leo von Klenze. München 1964

Herbert Brunner: Chinesisches Porzellan im Residenzmuseum München. München 1966

Rainer Rückert: Katalog der Ausstellung »Meißener Porzellan 1710-1810«. München 1966

Adalbert von Bayern: Als die Residenz noch Residenz war. München 1966

Brigitte Knüttel: Zur Geschichte der Münchner Residenz 1600-1616. In: Münchner Jahrbuch der bildenden Kunst 3. F. 18, 1967, S. 187-210

Ulla Krempel: Augsburger und Münchner Emailarbeiten aus dem Besitz der bayerischen Herzöge... In: Müchner Jahrbuch der bildenden Kunst 3. F. 18, 1967, S. 111-186

Heinrich Kreisel: Die Kunst des deutschen Möbels. 3 Bde (Bd. 3 von Georg Himmelheber). München 1968-1973

Otto Meitinger: Die baugeschichtliche Entwicklung der Neuveste. In: Oberbayerisches Archiv 92, 1970, S. 1-295

Herbert Brunner: Reliquienkronen aus der Münchener Reichen Kapelle. In: Zeitschrift für bayerische Landesgeschichte 35, 1972, S. 86-99

Liselotte Andersen: Eine unbekannte Quellenschrift aus der Zeit um 1700. In: Münchner Jahrbuch der bildenden Kunst 3. F. 24, 1973, S. 175-237

André Boutemy: Analyses... de meubles français anonymes du XVIIIe siècle. Brüssel 1973

Norbert Lieb und Heinz Jürgen Sauermost (Hrsg.): Münchens Kirchen. München 1973

Gerhard Hojer: Königliches Porzellan aus Nymphenburg. In: Weltkunst 44, 1974, S. 1782-1783

Eveline Schlumberger: La Résidence de Munich - une restauration magnifique. In: Connaissance des arts 267, Mai 1974, S. 108-119

Michael D. Grünwald: Christoph Angermair - Studien zu Leben und Werk des Elfenbein-schnitzers und Bildhauers. München/Zürich 1975

Katalog der Ausstellung »Kurfürst Max Emanuel - Bayern und Europa um 1700«. 2 Bde. München 1976

Brigitte Volk-Knüttel: Wandteppiche für den Münchner Hof nach Entwürfen von Peter Candid. München 1976

Klaus Maurice: Die deutsche Räderuhr. 2 Bde. München 1976

Herbert Brunner: Die Kunstschätze der Münchner Residenz. Hrsg. von Albrecht Miller. München 1977

Hans Ottomeyer: Eine königliche Wohnung wird möbliert. In: Weltkunst 47, 1977, S. 390-392

Hans Ottomeyer: Bronzekunst 1720-1880. In: Weltkunst 47, 1977, S. 2155-2159

Christina Thon: J. B. Zimmermann als Stukkator. München/Zürich 1977

Inken Nowald: Die Nibelungenfresken von Julius Schnorr von Carolsfeld im Königsbau der Münchner Residenz 1827-1867. Kiel 1978

Heinrich Geissler: Neues zu Friedrich Sustris. In: Münchner Jahrbuch der bildenden Kunst 3. F. 29, 1978, S. 65-91

Hans Ottomeyer: Die klassizistischen Uhren in der Münchner Residenz und in Schloß Nymphenburg. In: Alte Uhren 2, 1978, S. 161-180

Georg Baumgartner und Lorenz Seelig: Katalog der Ausstellung »Der Bayerische Hausritterorden vom Hl. Georg 1729-1979«. München 1979

Hans Ottomeyer: Das Wittelsbacher Album. Interieurs königlicher Wohn- und Festräume 1799-1848. München 1979

Luigi Zangheri: La grotta nella residenza di Monaco di Baviera: In: Antichità viva 4, 1979, S. 45-49

Toni Beil: Der Königsbau der Münchener Residenz. In: Jahrbuch der bayerischen Denkmalpflege 33, 1979, S. 199-212

Kataloge der Ausstellungen »Wittelsbach und Bayern« II und III, 4 Bde. München 1980

Quellen und Studien zur Kunstpolitik der Wittelsbacher vom 16. bis 18. Jahrhundert. Hrsg. von Hubert Glaser. München 1980

Katalog der Ausstellung   »Glyptothek München 1830-1980«. München 1980 (darin u.a. Heike Frosien-Leinz: Das Antiquarium der Residenz und Gerhard Hojer: Die Skulpturen der Glyptothek auf Nymphenburger Porzellan)

Gerhard Hojer, Elmar D. Schmid, Lorenz Seelig: Residenzmuseum München (Reihe »museum«). Braunschweig 1980

Gerhard Hojer: Die Münchner Residenz um 1800. In: Weltkunst 50, 1980, S. 690-694

Lorenz Seelig: Ein Deckenbildentwurf für die Grüne Galerie der Münchner Residenz. In: Weltkunst 50, 1980, S. 3647-3649

Hans Ottomeyer: »Amor und Psyche« von Martin-Claude Monot. Fundberichte zur Geschichte eines ungewöhnlichen Ensembles (1781/82). In: Pantheon 38, 1980, S. 263-269

Horst H. Stierhof: Die Münchner Residenz. In: Bayerland 82, Nr. 4, 1980, S. 2-30.

Helmut Seling: Die Kunst der Augsburger Goldschmiede 1529-1868. 3 Bde. München 1980

Rainer Rückert: Wittelsbacher Porzellane, Teil III: Porträts der Familie des Königs Murat von Raffaele Giovine auf einem neapolitanischen Vasensatz von 1814. In: Kunst und Antiquitäten 3, 1980, S. 20-35

Veronika Schaefer: Leo von Klenze. Möbel und Innenräume. München 1980

Eva-Maria Wasem: Die Münchener Residenz unter Ludwig I. Bildprogramme und Bildausstattungen in den Neubauten. München 1981

Cornelia Kemp: Das Herzkabinett der Kurfürstin Henriette Adelaide in der Münchner Residenz. In: Münchner Jahrbuch der bildenden Kunst 3. F. 33, 1982, S. 131-154

Hans Ottomeyer und Lorenz Seelig: Das Silber- und Vermeil-Service König Jérômes von West-falen in der Münchner Residenz. In: Münchner Jahrbuch der bildenden Kunst 3. F. 34, 1983, S. 117-164

Lorenz Seelig: Katalog der Ausstellung »Kirchliche Schätze aus bayerischen Schlössern. Liturgische Gewänder und Geräte des 16. - 19. Jahrhunderts«. München 1984

Lorenz Seelig: Farbige Einlegearbeiten aus Stein und Stuck in Münchner Schlössern. In: Schöndruck - Widerdruck. Schriften-Fest für Michael Meier zum 20. Dezember 1985. München/Berlin 1985, S. 28-45

Lorenz Seelig: Eine Pendule Charles Cressents. Vergoldete Bronzen in der Grünen Galerie der Münchner Residenz. In: Kunst & Antiquitäten 5, 1985, S. 42-45

Mario-Andreas von Lüttichau: Fürstenbildnisse in der Residenz in München. In: Weltkunst 55, 1985, S. 1870-1874

Hans Ottomeyer und Peter Pröschel: Vergoldete Bronzen. Die Bronzearbeiten des Spätbarock und Klassizismus. 2 Bde. München 1986

Wolfgang Braunfels: François Cuvilliés. Der Baumeister der galanten Architektur des Rokoko. München 1986

Elmar D. Schmid: Der Wintergarten König Ludwigs II. in der Münchner Residenz. In: Gerhard Hojer (Hrsg.): König Ludwig II. - Museum Herrenchiemsee. Katalog, München 1986, S.63-94

Dorothea Diemer: Bronzeplastik um 1600 in München. Neue Quellen und Forschun-gen. In: Jahrbuch des Zentralinstituts für Kunstgeschichte 2, 1986, S. 107-177 und 3, 1987, S. 109-168

Ellen Weski und Heike Frosien-Leinz (mit Beiträgen von Wolf-Dieter Grimm, Gerhard Hojer, Josef Riederer, Ulrich Schießl, Lorenz Seelig und Horst H. Stierhof): Das Antiquarium der Münchner Residenz. Katalog der Skulpturen. 2 Bde. München 1987

Michaela Liebhardt: Die Münchner Scagliolaarbeiten des 17. und 18. Jahrhunderts. Dissertation München 1987

Lorenz Seelig: Scagliola und Pietradura. Farbige Stein-und Stuckintarsien in Münch-ner Schlössern und Museen. In: Kunst & Antiquitäten 1, 1987, S. 26-39

Tino Walz, Otto Meitinger und Toni Beil: Die Residenz zu München. Entstehung - Zerstörung - Wiederaufbau (= Bavaria Antiqua). München 1987

Adrain von Buttlar und Traudl Bierler-Rolly (Hrsg.): Der Münchner Hofgarten. Beiträge zur Spurensicherung. München 1988

Denkmäler am Münchner Hofgarten. Forschungen und Berichte zu Planungsgeschichte und historischem Baubestand (= Arbeitsheft 41 des Bayerischen Lande-samtes für Denkmalpflege). München 1988

Gabriele Dischinger: Ein Augsburger Plan für das Münchner Antiquarium. In: Oberbayerisches Archiv 112, 1988, S. 81-86

Lorenz Seelig: Münchner Stickereien des 18. Jahrhunderts. In: Kunst & Antiquitäten 3, 1988, S. 72-80

Hermann Bauer und Bernhard Rupprecht: Corpus der barocken Deckenmalerei in Deutschland. Bd. 3/II. Stadt und Landkreis München. Profanbauten. Bearbeitet von Anna Bauer-Wild und Brigitte Volk-Knüttel. München 1989

Katharina Grundmann: Das KPM-Service für Maximilian II. in der Münchner Residenz. In: Keramos 125, 1989, S. 11-80

Burkard von Roda: »... doch dass es sich gut putzen lasset...«. Das Bamberger Tafelservice, Augsburger Silberarbeiten des 18. Jahrhunderts. In: Kunst & Antiquitäten 4, 1989, S. 66-73

Lorenz Seelig: Die Münchner Kunstkammer. Geschichte, Anlage, Ausstattung. In: Jahrbuch der bayerischen Denkmalpflege 40, 1986 (erschienen 1989), S. 101-138

Lorenz Seelig: Die vergoldeten Bronzen im Königsbau der Münchner Residenz. In: Jahrbuch des Zentralinstituts für Kunstgeschichte, Bd. V/VI, 1989/1990, S. 379-440

Georg Dehio: Handbuch der Deutschen Kunstdenkmäler. Bayern IV: München und Oberbayern. München 1990 (Residenz S. 738-760)

Gerhard Hojer: Die Prunkappartements Ludwigs I. im Königsbau der Münchner Residenz. Architektur und Dekoration. München 1992

Samuel John Klingensmith: The Utility of Splendor. Ceremony, Social Life and Architecture at the Court of Bavaria, 1600-1800. Ed. by Christian F. Otto und Mark Ashton. Chicago/London 1993

Sabine Heym: Silberkammer - Schatzkammer - Reiche Kapelle. Augsburger Goldschmiedekunst in der Münchner Residenz. In: Ausstellungskatalog »Silber und Gold I. Augsburger Goldschmiedekunst für die Höfe Europas« (Bayerisches Nationalmuseum München). München 1994, S. 83-101

Brigitte Langer: Mobilier français de la Résidence de Munich. In: Connaissance des Arts 512, 1994, S. 76-85

Dorothea und Peter Diemer: Das Antiquarium Herzog Albrechts V. von Bayern. Schicksale einer fürstlichen Antikensammlung der Spätrenaissance. In: Zeitschrift für Kunstgeschichte 58, H. 1, 1995, S. 55-104

Sabine Heym: Das Alte Residenztheater/Cuvilliés-Theater in München. München 1995

Brigitte Langer: Die Möbel der Residenz München Bd. I. Die französischen Möbel des 18. Jahrhunderts. Hrsg. von Gerhard Hojer und Hans Ottomeyer. München/New York 1995

Anne de La Tour d' Auvergne: Lapis Specularis. Scagliole of the Reiche Kapelle. In: FMR 77, 1995, S. 29-60

Afra Schick: Cuvilliés-Konsoltische. Anzahl und Aufstellung in der Grünen Galerie der Münchner Residenz. In: Weltkunst 22, 1995, S. 3230-3231

INDEX OF ARTISTS AND ARTISANS

INDEX OF ILLUSTRATIONS

Cover: Fountain Courtyard with the Wittelsbach Fountain

M · D C · XVI

PATRONA
BOIARIÆ

2

6

OPTAT ANAS MEDIIS CLAVARVM VERBER IN VNDIS,
CVM VIDET, VNGVIGERAS IN SVA FATA MINAS.

11

13

ANDESHVTVM OPIDVM ET ARCEM IN
ONTE ADIACENTE SEDEM DVCALEM
ÆDIFICAT. AN.M.CLXXXIII.

16

19

20

25

27

28

31

33

34

39

40

	Bayerische Verwaltung der staatlichen Schlösser, Gärten und Seen	

SEHENSWÜRDIGKEITEN

Ansbach	**Residenz der Markgrafen von Ansbach;** Prunkappartements des frühen Rokoko, Sammlung Ansbacher Fayencen und Porzellan, Hofgarten mit Orangerie	Tel. 0981/3186 Fax 0981/95840
Aschaffenburg	**Schloß Johannisburg** Gemäldegalerie und Kurfürstliche Wohnräume, Sammlung von Korkmodellen, Schloßgarten; Städtisches Schloßmuseum	Tel. 06021/22417 Fax 06021/218921
	Pompejanum; Nachbildung eines römischen Hauses und Antikenmuseum	
	Schloß und Park Schönbusch Klassizistisches Schlößchen in englischem Landschaftsgarten	
Bamberg	**Neue Residenz Bamberg** Kaisersaal und barocke Prunkräume, Gemäldegalerie, Rosengarten	Tel. 0951/56351 Fax 0951/55923
Bayreuth	**Neues Schloß** Markgrafenresidenz aus der Zeit des »Bayreuther Rokoko« mit Museum Bayreuther Fayencen, Hofgarten mit Orangerie	Tel. 0921/75969-0 Fax 0921/75969-15
	Markgräfliches Opernhaus	
Bayreuth/ Donndorf	**Schloßpark Fantaisie** Historische Gartenanlage	Tel. 0921/75969-0 Fax 0921/75969-15

Bayreuth/ Eremitage	**Altes Schloß Eremitage** Wohnräume der Markgräfin Wilhelmine, Grotte, historische Gartenanlage mit Wasser- spielen	Tel. 0921/75969-0 Fax 0921/75969-15
Bayreuth/ Wonsees Sanspareil	**Morgenländischer Bau** Stilräume, Gartenparterre und Felsengarten **Burg Zwernitz,** Burganlage	Tel. 0921/75969-0 Fax 0921/75969-15
Burghausen	**Burg zu Burghausen** Burganlage, Stilräume, Gemäldegalerie	Tel. 08677/4659 Fax 08677/65674
Coburg	**Schloß Ehrenburg** Historische Wohn- und Prunkräume des Barock und 19. Jahrhunderts	Tel. 09561/8088-0 Fax 09561/8088-40
Coburg/ Rödental	**Schloß Rosenau** in englischem Landschafts- garten, Wohnräume der Biedermeierzeit und neu- gotischer Marmorsaal	Tel. 09563/4747 Fax 09561/8088-40
Dachau	**Schloß Dachau;** Festsaal, historische Gartenanlage	Tel. 08131/87923 Fax 08131/78573
Eichstätt	**Willibaldsburg** Festungsanlage, Juramuseum, Ur- und Frühgeschichtsmu- seum, Hortus Eystettensis	Tel. 08421/4730 Fax 08421/8194
Ellingen	**Residenz Ellingen;** Prunk- appartements des Fürsten Wrede, Deutschordensräume, Schloßkirche, historische Gartenanlage	Tel. 09141/3327 Fax 09141/72953

Herrenchiemsee	**Neues Schloß**	Tel. 08051/6887-0
	Herrenchiemsee	Fax 08051/6887-99
	Wohn- und Repräsentations-	
	räume, historische Gartenan-	
	lage mit Wasserspielen und	
	König Ludwig II. Museum	
	Museum im Alten Schloß	
	Dauerausstellung zur ehema-	
	ligen Klosteranlage und zum	
	Verfassungskonvent; Stilräume	
	König Ludwigs II.	
Höchstädt	**Schloß Höchstädt**	Tel. 08431/8897
	Kapelle mit Sammlung	Fax 08431/42689
	südwestdeutscher Fayencen	
Kelheim	**Befreiungshalle**	Tel./Fax 09441/1584
Kempten	**Residenz Kempten**	Tel. 0831/256-1
	Prunkräume und Thronsaal	und 0831/256-251
	der Fürstäbte	Fax 0831/256-260
Königssee	**St. Bartholomä;** Jagdschloß,	Tel. 08652/96360
	Kapelle St. Johann und Paul,	Fax 08652/64721
	Naturpark Berchtesgaden	
Kulmbach	**Plassenburg;** Schöner Hof,	Tel. 09221/4116
	historische Markgrafenzimmer,	
	Gemäldegalerie, Jagdwaffen-	
	sammlung	
Landshut	**Stadtresidenz;** Stilräume und	Tel. 0871/92411-0
	Gemäldegalerie, Kreis- und	und 0871/92411-44
	Stadtmuseum	Fax 0871/92411-40
	Burg Trausnitz	
	Burganlage mit Burgkapelle	
	St. Georg, Stilräume	
Lauenstein bei	**Burg Lauenstein**	Tel./Fax 09263/400
Ludwigsstadt	Burganlage, Wohnräume,	
	volkskundliche Sammlungen	

Linderhof	**Schloß Linderhof**	Tel. 08822/9203-0
	Wohn- und Repräsentations-	Fax 08822/9203-11
	räume, Venusgrotte, Marokka-	
	nisches Haus, Maurischer Kiosk	
	und Hundinghütte, historische	
	Gartenanlage mit Wasser-	
	spielen	

München

Residenzmuseum   Tel. 089/29067-1
Historische Wohn- und Prunk- Fax 089/29067-225
räume aus der Zeit der Renais-
sance bis zum 19. Jahrhundert,
Hofkirchen und -kapellen, Spe-
zialsammlungen (Silber, Porzellan, Paramente, Reliquien)

Schatzkammer

Altes Residenztheater
(Cuvilliés-Theater)

Hofgarten

Bavaria mit Ruhmeshalle
auf der Theresienhöhe

Schloß Nymphenburg   Tel. 089/17908-0
Prunk- und Stilräume, Festsaal, Fax 089/17908-627
Schönheitengalerie, Schloß-
kapelle

**Amalienburg, Badenburg, Pa-
godenburg, Magdalenenklause**
im historischen Schloßpark

Marstallmuseum
Höfische Kutschen und Schlit-
ten, Reit- und Sattelzeug

**Museum Nymphenburger
Porzellan**
Sammlung Bäuml

	Englischer Garten Landschaftsgarten im englischen Stil	Tel. 089/341986 Fax 089/335169
München/ Oberschleißheim	**Neues Schloß Schleißheim** Festsäle, Staatsappartements, Gemäldegalerie, barocker Hof- garten	Tel. 089/315872-0 Fax 089/315872-50
	Schloß Lustheim Porzellansammlung	
Neuburg a.d. Donau	**Schloßmuseum** **Neuburg a.d. Donau** Sgraffitofassade, Kapelle, Grotten; Vorgeschichte Pfalz- Neuburg, Kirchlicher Barock	Tel. 08431/8897 Fax 08431/42689
Neuschwanstein/ Schwangau	**Schloß Neuschwanstein** Wohn- und Repräsentations- räume	Tel. 08362/81035 und 08362/81801 Fax 08362/8990
Nürnberg	**Kaiserburg Nürnberg** Palas, Stilräume, Doppel- kapelle, Tiefer Brunnen und Sinwellturm, Burggarten	Tel. 0911/225726 Fax 0911/2059117
Prunn im Altmühltal	**Burg Prunn** Stilräume	Tel. 09442/3323 Fax 09442/3335
Riedenburg	**Burg Rosenburg** Burganlage mit Kapelle; privat betriebener Falkenhof	Tel. 09442/2752 Fax 09442/3287
Schachen	**Königshaus am Schachen** Wohnräume und Maurischer Saal, Alpengarten	Tel. 08821/2996
Schnaittach	**Festung Rothenberg** Ruine einer Festungsanlage aus dem 18. Jahrhundert	Tel. 09153/7793

Übersee/Feldwies	**Künstlerhaus Exter** mit Atelier des Malers Julius Exter	Tel. 08642/8950-83 Fax 08642/8950-85
Utting am Ammersee	**Künstlerhaus Gasteiger** Sommervilla mit Wohnräumen und Werken von Anna und Mathias Gasteiger, Villengarten	Tel. 08806/2682 und 08806/2091
Veitshöchheim	**Schloß und Park Veitshöchheim;** Historische Wohnräume, Rokokogarten mit Wasserspielen	Tel. 0931/91582 Fax 0931/51925
Würzburg	**Residenz Würzburg;** Barocke Prunkräume, Fresken von G.B. Tiepolo, Gemäldegalerie, Hofgarten	Tel. 0931/355170 Fax 0931/51925
	Festung Marienberg Festungsanlage, Fürstenbaumuseum mit Schatzkammer, Paramentensaal und stadtgeschichtliche Sammlungen, Maschikuliturm, Fürstengarten; Mainfränkisches Museum	

Veröffentlichungen
der Bayerischen Verwaltung der staatlichen Schlösser, Gärten und Seen

Amtliche Führer   **je DM 4,00 – 6,00**
Deutsche Ausgaben:

Ansbach	Residenz Ansbach
Aschaffenburg	Schloß Aschaffenburg
	Pompejanum in Aschaffenburg
	Schloß und Park Schönbusch
Bamberg	Neue Residenz Bamberg
Bayreuth	Eremitage zu Bayreuth
	Markgräfliches Opernhaus Bayreuth
	Neues Schloß Bayreuth
Bayreuth/Wonsees	Felsengarten Sanspareil – Burg Zwernitz
Burghausen	Burg zu Burghausen
Coburg	Coburg - Schloß Ehrenburg
Coburg/Rödental	Schloß Rosenau
Dachau	Schloß Dachau
Eichstätt	Willibaldsburg Eichstätt
Ellingen	Residenz Ellingen
Herrenchiemsee	Neues Schloß Herrenchiemsee
Kelheim	Befreiungshalle Kelheim
Königssee	St. Bartholomä am Königssee
Kulmbach ·	Plassenburg ob Kulmbach
Landshut	Landshut Burg Trausnitz
	Stadtresidenz Landshut
Lauenstein bei Ludwigsstadt	Burg Lauenstein
Linderhof	Schloß Linderhof
München	Residenz München
	Schatzkammer der Residenz München
	Altes Residenztheater in München
	(Cuvilliés-Theater)
	Englischer Garten München
	Ruhmeshalle und Bavaria
	Nymphenburg, Schloß, Park und Burgen
	Marstallmuseum in Schloß Nymphenburg
Neuburg a. d. Donau	Schloßmuseum Neuburg an der Donau
Neuschwanstein/Schwangau	Schloß Neuschwanstein
Nürnberg	Kaiserburg Nürnberg
Oberschleißheim	Schloß Schleißheim, Neues Schloß und Garten

Prunn	Burg Prunn
Riedenburg	Burg Rosenburg in Riedenburg an der Altmühl
Schachen	Königshaus am Schachen
Veitshöchheim	Veitshöchheim
Würzburg	Festung Marienberg zu Würzburg
	Residenz Würzburg und Hofgarten

English Editions:

Aschaffenburg	Aschaffenburg Castle
Bayreuth	The Hermitage at Bayreuth
	Margravial Opera House Bayreuth
Coburg	Coburg Ehrenburg Palace
Herrenchiemsee	The New Palace of Herrenchiemsee
Linderhof	Linderhof Palace
München	Residence Munich
	The Treasury in the Munich Residence
	Nymphenburg, Palace, Park, Pavilions
	Marstallmuseum Schloß Nymphenburg in Munich
Neuschwanstein/Schwangau	Neuschwanstein Castle
Nürnberg	Imperial Castle Nuremberg
Schachen	The Royal House on the Schachen
Würzburg	The Würzburg Residence and Court Gardens

Editions with English Summary:

Bamberg	Neue Residenz Bamberg
Bayreuth/Wonsees	Felsengarten Sanspareil - Burg Zwernitz
Burghausen	Burg zu Burghausen
Coburg/Rödental	Schloß Rosenau
Königssee	St. Bartholomä am Königssee
München	Englischer Garten München
Oberschleißheim	Schloß Schleißheim

Editions Françaises:

Herrenchiemsee	Le Nouveau Château de Herrenchiemsee
Linderhof	Le Château de Linderhof
München	Le Trésor de la Résidence de Munich
	Nymphenburg, Le Château, le Parc et les Pavillons
Neuschwanstein/Schwangau	Le Château de Neuschwanstein
Nürnberg	Le Château Impérial de Nuremberg

Schachen   Le Châlet Royal de Schachen
Würzburg   Wurtzbourg, Le Palais des Princes
                    Évêques et les Jardins

Editions avec résumé français:
Bayreuth/Wonsees   Felsengarten Sanspareil - Burg Zwernitz
München   Englischer Garten München

Edizioni Italiane:
Herrenchiemsee   Castello di Herrenchiemsee
Linderhof   Castello di Linderhof
München   Tesoro della Residenz München
                                Nymphenburg, II Castello, il Parco
                                e i Castelli del Giardino
Neuschwanstein/Schwangau Castello di Neuschwanstein
Würzburg   La Residenza di Würzburg e il Giardino di
                                Corte

Japanische Ausgaben:
Herrenchiemsee   Schloß Herrenchiemsee
Linderhof   Schloß Linderhof
München   Nymphenburg
Neuschwanstein/Schwangau Schloß Neuschwanstein
Würzburg   Residenz Würzburg und Hofgarten

Prospekte und Zeitschriften

Prospekt »**Ansbacher Fayencen**«	DM 1,00
Prospekt »**Nymphenburger Porzellan – Sammlung Bäuml**«	DM 1,50
Prospekt »**Königshaus am Schachen**«	DM 1,50
Prospekt »**Residenz Kempten** (dt., engl.)«	DM 2,00
Prospekt »**Schloßpark Linderhof**«	DM 2,00
Broschüre »**Staatliche Schlösser und Gärten in Bayern –** **Besucherinformation 1999**«, (deutsch/englisch) – erhältlich gegen Einsendung von DM 5,– in Briefmarken –	DM 3,00

Museumspädagogische Schriften

Schloß Nymphenburg entdecken (1994)	DM 6,00

Bildhefte der Bayerischen Schlösserverwaltung

Heft 1: *Heym, Sabine:* **Das Alte Residenztheater/Cuvilliés-** **Theater in München** (dt., engl., frz., ital.); München 1995	DM 15,00
Heft 2: *Heym, Sabine:* **Amadis und Oriane – Im Zauberreich** **der barocken Oper.** Tapisserien im Neuen Schloß Bayreuth, München 1998	DM 9,00

Reihe »Forschungen zur Kunst- und Kulturgeschichte«

Band I: *Sangl, Sigrid:* **Das Bamberger Hofschreinerhandwerk** **im 18. Jahrhundert;** München 1990 (kartoniert)	DM 30,00
Band II: *Hojer, Gerhard:* **Die Prunkappartements Ludwigs I.** **im Königsbau der Münchner Residenz;** München 1992 (kartoniert)	DM 35,00
Band III: *Stierhof Horst H.:* »**das biblisch gemäl**«. Die Kapelle im Ottheinrichsbau des Schlosses Neuburg an der Donau; München 1993 (broschiert)	DM 12,00
Band IV: *Störkel, Arno:* **Christian Friedrich Carl Alexander.** Der letzte Markgraf von Ansbach-Bayreuth, 2. Auflage, im Bild- teil ergänzt und erweitert; Ansbach 1998 (kartoniert)	DM 38,00
Band V: *Hojer, Gerhard* (Hrsg.): **Bayerische Schlösser –** **Bewahren und Erforschen;** München 1996 (kartoniert)	DM 48,00
Band VI: *Toussaint, Ingo:* **Lustgärten um Bayreuth.** Eremitage, Sanspareil und Fantaisie in Beschreibungen aus dem 18. und 19. Jahrhundert; Georg Olms Verlag, Hildesheim 1998 (kartoniert)	DM 68,00

Reihe »Baudokumentationen«

o.Nr.: *Land- und Universitätsbauamt Augsburg im Auftrag der Bayeri-*
schen Verwaltung der staatlichen Schlösser, Gärten und Seen (Hrsg.):
Restaurierung Schloß Höchstädt, Festschrift zur Fertigstellung des
I. Bauabschnitts und zur Eröffnung der Fayencenausstellung am
19. Oktober 1995 (broschiert)   DM 6,00

o.Nr.: *Landbauamt Rosenheim im Auftrag der Bayerischen Verwaltung*
der staatlichen Schlösser, Gärten und Seen (Hrsg.)::: **Wasserspiele**
Herrenchiemsee, Festschrift 1994 (broschiert)   DM 15,00

Heft 1: *Staatliches Hochbauamt Weilheim im Auftrag der Bayerischen*
Verwaltung der staatlichen Schlösser, Gärten und Seen (Hrsg.): **Das**
Marokkanische Haus im Schloßpark Linderhof.
– Band I; Bildheft (broschiert)   *ca. DM 15,00*
Erscheinungstermin: Sommer 1999
– Band II; Dokumentation zur Wiedererrichtung
und Restaurierung (broschiert)   DM 20,00

Ausstellungskataloge und -Broschüren

Bayerische Verwaltung der staatlichen Schlösser, Gärten und Seen
(Hrsg.): **200 Jahre Englischer Garten München 1789–1989;**
München 1989 (broschiert)   DM 4,00

Bayerische Verwaltung der staatlichen Schlösser, Gärten und Seen
(Hrsg.): **Hortus Eystettensis – ein vergessener Garten?;**
München 1998 (broschiert)   DM 8,00

Krückmann, Peter O. (Bearb.): **Carlo Carlone 1686–1775.**
Der Ansbacher Auftrag (kartoniert); Arcos/Landshut 1990   DM 37,00
(Buchhandelspreis: DM 79,00)

Krückmann, Peter O. (Hrsg.): **Der Himmel auf Erden –**
Tiepolo in Würzburg. Band I Ausstellungskatalog.   Bd. I: DM 39,00
Band II Aufsätze: Prestel, München/New York 1996   Bd. II: vergriffen
(broschiert)
(Buchhandelspreise/Leinen: Band I DM 78,00;
Band II DM 86,00; Band I+II DM 148,00)

Krückmann, Peter O.: **Heaven on Earth – Tiepolo – Masterpieces**
of the Würzburg Years; Prestel, München/New York 1996
(broschiert)   DM 78,00

Krückmann, Peter O.: **Paradies des Rokoko,**
Band I Das Bayreuth der Markgräfin Wilhelmine   Bd. I: DM 39,00
Band II Galli Bibiena und der Musenhof der   Bd. II: DM 65,00
Wilhelmine von Bayreuth/Ausstellungskatalog;   Bd. I+II: DM 92,00
Prestel, München/New York 1998 (broschiert)
(Buchhandelspreise/Leinen: Band I DM 78,00;
Band II DM 86,00; Band I+II DM 148,00)

Schmid, Elmar D. und *Sabine Heym* (Bearb.): **Josef Effner 1687–1745.**
  Bauten für Kurfürst Max Emanuel; München 1987 (broschiert)   DM 2,00
Schmid, Elmar D. (Bearb.): **Friedrich Wilhelm Pfeiffer 1822–1891.**
  Maler der Reitpferde König Ludwigs II.; Bayerland,
  Dachau 1988 (kartoniert)   DM 32,00
Schmid, Elmar D. und *Sabine Heym* (Bearb.): **Mathias und Anna
  Gasteiger.** Aus einem Münchner Künstlerleben um 1900;
  Bayerland, Dachau 1985 (broschiert)   DM 15,00
Schmid, Elmar D.: **Der Krönungswagen Kaiser Karls VII.** Wahl und
  Krönung in Frankfurt am Main 1742; Bayerland, Dachau 1992
  (broschiert)   DM 25,00
Schmid, Elmar D.: **König Ludwig II. im Portrait;**
  Bayerland, Dachau 1996 (Leinen)   DM 68,00
Schmid, Elmar D.: **Julius Exter – Unbekannte Werke aus dem
  Nachlaß seiner Schülerin Olga Fritz-Zetter;** München 1996
  (broschiert)   DM 10,00
Schmid, Elmar D.: **Julius Exter – Aufbruch in die Moderne;**
  Klinkhardt & Biermann, München/Berlin 1998 (broschiert)   DM 48,00
  (Buchhandelspreis/Leinen: DM 98,00)
Stierhof, Horst H.: »**das biblisch gemäl**«. 450 Jahre Schloß-
  kapelle Neuburg an der Donau; München 1993 (broschiert)   DM 5,00

Bestandskataloge

Frosien-Leinz, Heike und *Ellen Weski* (Bearb.): **Das Antiquarium
  der Münchner Residenz,** Katalog der Skulpturen. 2 Bände;
  Hirmer, München 1987 (Leinen)
  – nur im Buchhandel erhältlich –
Helmberger, Werner und *Valentin Kockel* (Bearb.): **Rom über die
  Alpen tragen.** Fürsten sammeln antike Architektur. Die Aschaffen-
  burger Korkmodelle; Arcos, Landshut 1993 (kartoniert)   DM 29,00
  (Buchhandelspreis: DM 59,50)
Hojer, Gerhard (Hrsg.): **König Ludwig II.-Museum Herren-
  chiemsee, Katalog;** Hirmer, München 1986 (kartoniert)   DM 35,00
  (Buchhandelspreis: DM 48,00)
Langer, Brigitte: **Die Möbel der Residenz München, Band 1.** Die
  französischen Möbel des 18. Jahrhunderts, hrsg. von Gerhard
  Hojer und Hans Ottomeyer; Prestel, München/New York 1995
  (broschiert)   DM 118,00
  (Buchhandelspreis/Leinen: DM 228,00)

Langer, Brigitte und *Alexander Herzog von Württemberg:* **Die Möbel der Residenz München, Band 2.** Die deutschen Möbel des 16. bis 18. Jahrhunderts, hrsg. von Gerhard Hojer und Hans Ottomeyer; Prestel, München/New York 1996 (broschiert)   DM 118,00
(Buchhandelspreis/Leinen: DM 228,00)

Langer, Brigitte, Hans Ottomeyer und *Alexander Herzog von Württemberg:* **Die Möbel der Residenz München, Band 3.** Möbel des Empire, Biedermeier und Spätklassizismus, hrsg. von Gerhard Hojer und Hans Ottomeyer; Prestel, München/New York 1997 (broschiert)   DM 118,00
(Buchhandelspreis/Leinen: DM 228,00)

Miller, Albrecht (Bearb.): **Bayreuther Fayencen;** Arcos, Landshut 1994 (kartoniert)   DM 28,00
(Buchhandelspreis: DM 49,80)

Seelig, Lorenz: **Kirchliche Schätze aus bayerischen Schlössern.** Liturgische Gewände und Geräte des 16. bis 19. Jahrhunderts; Deutscher Kunstverlag, Berlin 1984 (broschiert)   DM 10,00

Ziffer, Alfred: **Nymphenburger Porzellan.** Die Sammlung Bäuml/Bäuml Collection; Arnoldsche, Stuttgart 1996 (broschiert)   DM 98,00
(Buchhandelspreis/Leinen: DM 148,00)

Weitere Veröffentlichungen

Bayerische Verwaltung der staatlichen Schlösser, Gärten und Seen (Hrsg.): **Vierte Festschrift zum Wiederaufbau der Residenz München;** München 1959 (broschiert)   DM 5,00

Bayerische Verwaltung der staatlichen Schlösser, Gärten und Seen (Hrsg.): **Journal der Bayerischen Verwaltung der staatlichen Schlösser Gärten und Seen;** München 1995 (broschiert)   DM 10,00

Ermischer, Gerhard: **Schloßarchäologie – Funde zu Schloß Johannisburg in Aschaffenburg;** Museen der Stadt Aschaffenburg/Bayerische Schlösserverwaltung, Aschaffenburg 1996 (kartoniert)   DM 48,00

Facharbeitskreis Schlösser und Gärten in Deutschland (Hrsg.): **Reisezeit – Zeitreise zu den schönsten Schlössern, Burgen, Gärten, Klöstern und Römerbauten in Deutschland;** Schnell & Steiner, Regensburg 1999 (broschiert)   DM 16,80

Focht, Josef: **Die musische Aura der Markgräfin Wilhelmine.** Musikinszenierung in der Kunst des Bayreuther Rokoko; Peda, Passau 1998 (broschiert)   DM 17,80

Focht, Josef und *Hans Gurski:* **Das Gloria der Engel im Fürststift Kempten.** Musikdarstellungen in der Basilika St. Lorenz und der Residenz; Peda, Passau 1998 (broschiert)   DM 17,80

Heym, Sabine: **Feenreich und Ritterwelt – Die Rosenau als Ort romantisch-literarischen Welterlebens.** Sonderdruck aus »Bayerische Schlösser – Bewahren und Erforschen«; München 1996 (broschiert) — DM 4,00

Hojer, Gerhard (Hrsg.): **Der Italienische Bau.** Materialien und Untersuchungen zur Stadtresidenz Landshut; Arcos, Landshut 1994 (kartoniert) — DM 38,00

Hojer, Gerhard und *Peter O. Krückmann:* **Neues Schloß Bayreuth, Anton Raphael Mengs: »Königin Semiramis erhält die Nachricht vom Aufstand in Babylon«** (PATRIMONIA 49); Kulturstiftung der Länder und Bayerische Schlösserverwaltung, Berlin/München 1995 (broschiert) — DM 20,00

Kunz-Ott, Hannelore und *Andrea Kluge* (Hrsg.): **150 Jahre Feldherrnhalle.** Lebensraum einer Großstadt; Buchendorfer, München 1994 (broschiert) — DM 25,00

Kutschbach, Doris: **Tiepolo – Eine Reise um die Welt** (aus der Kinderbuch-Reihe »Abenteuer Kunst«); Prestel, München/New York 1996 (kartoniert) — DM 22,80

Langer, Brigitte: **Residenz München, zwei Kommoden des Bernard II Vanrisamburgh** (PATRIMONIA 134); Kulturstiftung der Länder und Bayerische Schlösserverwaltung, Berlin/München 1997 (broschiert) — DM 20,00

Lauterbach, Iris, Klaus Endemann und Christoph Luitpold Frommel (Hrsg.): **Die Landshuter Stadtresidenz.** Architektur und Ausstattung; Zentralinstitut für Kunstgeschichte (Band XIV), München 1998 (broschiert) — DM 48,00

Misslbeck-Woesler, Maria: **Die Flora des Englischen Gartens, München 1986** (kartoniert) — DM 15,00

Nickl, Peter (Hrsg.): **Parkett.** Historische Holzfußböden und zeitgenössische Parkettkultur; Klinkhardt & Biermann, München/Berlin 1995 (Leinen) — DM 78,00

Schmid, Elmar D.: **Das Exter-Haus** – Ein Künstlersitz am Chiemsee in Übersee-Feldwies; München 1997 (broschiert) — DM 10,00

Schuster, Rainer: **Nymphenburger Porzellan.** Kostbarkeiten aus der Sammlung Bäuml und dem Residenzmuseum München; München 1997 (broschiert) — DM 8,00

Schuster, Rainer: **Nymphenburg Porcelain.** Treasures from the Bäuml Collection and the Residence Museum Munich; München 1997 (broschiert) — DM 8,00

Stierhof, Horst H. (Bearb.): **Das Walhnhaus.** Der italienische Bau der Stadtresidenz Landshut; Landshut 1994 (broschiert) — DM 16,00

Werner, Ferdinand: **Der Hofgarten Veitshöchheim;** Wernersche, Worms 1998 (kartoniert) — DM 36,00

Plakate

groß (A 1):

Schlösserland Bayern	DM 7,00
König Ludwig II. (Portrait von Ferdinand Piloty, 1865)	DM 7,00
Nymphenburger Porzellan – Sammlung Bäuml	DM 7,00
Marstallmuseum	DM 7,00
Residenz München	DM 7,00
Schatzkammer der Residenz München	DM 7,00
Schloß Rosenau	DM 7,00
Schloß Ehrenburg Coburg	DM 7,00
Schloß und **Park Schönbusch**	DM 7,00
Bayreuther Fayencen (Sammlung Rummel)	DM 7,00
Landshut: **Burg Trausnitz** – **Stadtresidenz**	DM 7,00
Residenz Kempten	DM 7,00
»Rom über die Alpen tragen«	
(Korkmodelle in Schloß Johannisburg)	DM 5,00
Schloßmuseum Neuburg an der Donau	DM 5,00

klein (A 2/A 3)

Korkmodell **»Pantheon«** (Schloß Johannisburg)	DM 5,00
Pompejanum Aschaffenburg	DM 5,00
Neue Residenz Bamberg	DM 5,00
Plan **»Schloßpark Nymphenburg«**	DM 5,00
Ausstellungsplakat **»das biblisch gemäl«**	
(Schloßkapelle Neuburg)	DM 3,00
Ausstellungsplakat **»von denen schönen Gärten«**	
(Schloß Fantaisie)	DM 5,00
Ausstellungsplakat **»Hortus Eystettensis«**	
(Willibaldsburg Eichstätt)	DM 5,00

CD-ROM

Ludwig II. – Ich, der König.
Leben, Schlösser, Musik, Dynastie, Zeitgeschichte   DM 79,00
Ludwig II – I, the king.
Life, Castles, Music, Dynasty, Contemporary History   DM 79,00

Videos des Bayerischen Rundfunks

– **Nymphenburg, Schloß und Park** (PAL/dt.; NTSC/engl.)   DM 39,95
– **Die Kaiserburg in Nürnberg** (PAL/dt.)   DM 39,95
– **Die Königsschlösser** (PAL/dt., PAL/engl.; NTSC/engl.)   DM 39,95
  Das Video »Die Königsschlösser« gibt es in englischer
  Sprache in zwei verschiedenen Systemen: im PAL-System
  (z.B. für Großbritannien und Südafrika) und im
  NTSC-System (z.B. für USA, Kanada und Japan).
– **»Herr der sieben Länder« – Kurfürst Carl Theodor
  von Baiern und der Pfalz** (PAL/dt.)   DM 29,95

Ausstellungsvideos:

– **»Der Himmel auf Erden«** – Tiepolo in der Würzburger
  Residenz   DM 39,95
– **»Das vergessene Paradies«** – Galli Bibiena und der
  Musenhof der Wilhelmine von Bayreuth   DM 29,95

**Preise zzgl. Porto und Verpackung,
Bestellungen bitte an:
Bayerische Verwaltung der
staatlichen Schlösser, Gärten und Seen
Postfach 38 01 20, 80614 München
Tel: 089/17908-165; Fax 089/17908-154**